Decision Empowerment

A Parent's Guide to Raising Good Decision Makers

Robert N. Charette, Ph.D.
Brian W. Hagen, Ph.D.

dei Decision Empowerment Institute

Empower Decisions, Empower Lives

ISBN-13: 978-0-9795965-0-6
ISBN-10: 0-9795965-0-5

The following are Trademarks of the authors:
FIVE-to-Decide™; 5D ™; Look up, look down—then all the way around™; What makes the decision hard or tough? ™; What information is just enough? ™; What's good? What's bad? Let's ask Mom or Dad™; Let's do the math to find the best path™; Choose the best thing to do, and keep the promise true™; Little Decision Makers Ensemble™: Claire Smart-Choice™, Alan the Analyzer™, Debra Detail™, Frieda Fun Loving™, Skip the Quick™, Timothy Timid™, Browbeater Bill™, Anne the Advocate™, Davethe Decider™, Paul and Pauline Patience™; The Littlest Decision Makers™, The Little Decision Makers™, The Youngest Decision Maker™, The Young Decision Maker™, The Young Adult Decision Maker™, From Decision Impoverishment to Empowerment™, Decision Equity™; Decision Ladder™; Decision Factory™

9/28/07

To our children
Maura and Megan Charette
and
Koray and Altay Hagen

Who have inspired us to pursue decision empowerment
for all individuals, and especially children

And a special thank you to Koray Hagen
for writing Chapter 11, "Claire's Summary."

Dave -

I hope you find this familiar but refreshingly new!

Best Wishes,

Brian Hagen

Contents

Chapter 10—The Decide Dialogue: "Choose the best thing to do, and keep the promise true."

Chapter 11—Claire's Summary

PART III Putting It into Practice

Chapter 12—The Never-Ending Conversation

Preface

We're Blowing It . . . Big Time!

Do you remember those classroom discussions on decision making you had back in elementary school? Or the classes you took in middle school or high school? No? Well guess what. Chances are you didn't have any instruction on decision making other than the bedtime fables your parents read to you when you were three. In fact, most colleges and universities don't have them either. Or if they do, the classes require a significant math background as a prerequisite. How could a topic so profound to the human experience and so critical to every individual's success in life be so void from our educational system? We think this is WRONG!

We strongly believe that decision making should be part of the regular curriculum in school. That said, most school systems' curriculums are over-burdened now, their funding limited, and teaching decision making isn't on their short list of next fall's new curriculum. That is why it's so important that we as parents personally get involved in teaching our children this critical, life-time skill.

As parents, we have many responsibilities to our children. On top of providing them love and a comfortable and safe environment to grow up in, we want them to learn how to survive on their own. We want them to learn how to be individuals. We want them to learn how to think for themselves. We want them to learn how to be productive members of society. And most of all, we want them to be happy, healthy, and successful. And for those of you with high aspirations for your children, good decision-making skills is what differentiates leaders from successful leaders, innovators from successful innovators, and "want-to-be" entrepreneurs from successful entrepreneurs.

Children with superior decision-making skills will far surpass in life those without, everything else being equal. The very best gift you or I can give our children—if we want them to reach their full potential as adults—is to empower them in how to make high-quality decisions, especially when the potential consequences are great. But what do we mean by empower?

What This Book Is About

This book is about enabling *you*, as a parent, to empower your children to be superior decision makers—for the rest of their lives. Empowering your children to be superior decision makers requires two components. First, you must ensure your children acquire the skills needed to make high-quality decisions. Secondly, you must grant them, and they in turn accept, the authority to make decisions and the responsibility for the outcomes and consequences of their decisions.

About now you're probably asking yourself, "How can I empower my child to become a superior decision maker if she won't get those skills at school and I can't teach her because I wasn't properly trained myself?" We understand and appreciate your apprehension—but don't throw in the towel just yet. This is exactly why we were compelled to write this book. Our book gives you all the basic tools you need to teach your children (and yourself) how to make high quality decisions. We will tell you not only what to do, e.g., identifying the *right* decision, but also how to do it, and why you are doing it. And along the way we will show you how you can judiciously transfer authority and responsibility for decision making to your child as your child matures in judgment and increases their decision-making skills.

Since children learn best by doing, our approach centers on applying what we teach you—and then you to your children—in easily digestible steps. We have a little motto, *FIVE-to-Decide*™, that we use that will help remind you and your child what needs to be done and when. We have created other simple memory aids that break our motto into simple, learnable steps that even a young child can easily remember.

How Young Can I Start?

Most children reach a level of cognitive and emotional maturity for understanding the distinctions we are making in this book around the ages of 9 to 12. Putting all of these ideas into practice takes a level of sophistication, attention span, and reasoning skills not found in children of younger ages. Does this mean that we should begin our children's education on good decision making when they become adolescents? *Absolutely not!*

While 4 to 6 year olds really don't make any significant decisions (from a parent's perspective), you can help build the concepts and language so that by the time they reach ages 9 to 12 they are ready to have some "decision equity"—not decision empowerment. Decision equity means having some control over the decision including its associated choices but not full control over the ultimate decision and its consequences. Decision empowerment happens when you have 100 percent decision equity, a major goal that you should be training your child to reach eventually.

In fact, we believe that training your children to be able to assume confidently 100 percent decision empowerment is one of the best gifts you can bestow on them.

Benefits to Our Approach

Once our children are grown and out of the house, their success or failure will be based largely on three things: (1) the quality of the decisions you made for them; (2) the quality of the decisions our children made for themselves as they grew up, and most importantly, on; (3) the quality of the decisions our children then make in their careers and personal lives. We decided that a book grounded in the decision-making skills we teach professionals everyday—who also by the way often have trouble making quality decisions and drove us to write this book for our own children—are the most fitting for your children as well. In our conversations with corporate and government executives, the ability to make quality decisions is what separates those who get promoted from those who don't.

We believe that decision making is such an important skill that it would be a mistake to water the process down. However, we have provided an adult-appropriate approach to decision making that you can tailor for your child.

Beyond your children, we hope that the approaches you will learn in this book will make you a better collaborator in decision making with individuals—spouse, parents, business colleagues, and friends—that are important to you and your life.

So let's get started.

PART I

A Parent's Goal: Empowering Your Child to Be a Good Decision Maker

The Building Blocks of Decision Making

Starting Thoughts and Concepts:
Principles, Distinctions, and Language

Our decisions define our lives—not just the big decisions we make, such as who to marry or what career to pursue, but the many smaller day-to-day decisions that define the steps we take on our individual journeys. In fact, our lives are probably more the result of the accumulation of smaller, day-to-day decisions we make because they lead us to the crossroads in life, where the big decisions are made. Ultimately, the destinations we reach are the result of the accumulation of all of the decisions we make, both big and small. Our desire is that you and your children make the most of your lives by making the best possible decisions each step of the way. This chapter is devoted to the building blocks of decision making.

As we write this book, our children range in age from 18 months to 16 years. The youngest one is just now voicing her desires about what to eat while our eldest is trying to decide which classes to take to best position himself for keeping his options open for a university education. Between choosing what food to eat and university preparation decisions is a range of decisions, each growing in choices, complexity, and consequences.

As our children have grown, we have gradually increased their decision *equity* (the degree of control to make decisions on their own). At first, we limited the number and varieties of choices that we allowed our children to make and then loosened the constraints as they showed they could make quality decisions. The eldest is now at a point of fully understanding the concepts in this book and able to engage in high-quality decision conversations and has a high degree of autonomy in decision making. However, he still does not have full decision empowerment, meaning 100 percent decision equity for all decisions. Full or 100 percent decision equity—i.e., complete decision empowerment—means enjoying both the freedom to make decisions but also accepting the responsibility for the consequences of his decisions. We will talk more of this idea in the next chapter.

While they were young, we have tried to help our children learn to think broadly and systematically about the decisions they make and the choices they have to choose from associated with each decision. The possibilities of how to spend a Saturday afternoon with family are endless. It is not just watching TV, playing computer games, or going out for lunch. Being creative in identifying significantly different choices can be learned at an early age; and as we will see throughout this book, creativity is vitally important to becoming a skilled decision maker.

So far we've talked a lot about decision making, but what actually is this thing we call a decision?

What Is a Decision?

Simply put, a decision is a *commitment* of something of value (e.g., time or money). By saying a decision is a commitment, we mean that an explicit course of action has been chosen implying that we have forgone other possible courses of action. Choosing a single scoop chocolate ice cream cone implies that we are not having a vanilla ice cream cone, unless we're willing to pile on another scoop with all of those calories! During the car ride over to the ice cream parlor, we might discuss the various choices of ice cream cones; but the actual decision—commitment—comes at the time we pay the cashier for the ice cream. The bottom line is *if there is no commitment of a resource, then there is no decision.* This is a key distinction people often overlook and causes confusion and frustration in many conversations at home and at work. We've sat in many corporate meetings where decisions have been discussed—sometimes seemingly endlessly—but not made. Think about this in your next conversation involving decision making.

Decision Elements

Decisions consist of four components: (1) choices, (2) information, (3) values/preferences, and (4) consequences.

Choices include the set of various alternatives that we have to choose from (e.g., the different flavors of ice cream that the ice cream parlor usually offers).

Information includes the facts and events (both certain and uncertain) that affect our choices and how we value *consequences* (e.g., what flavors of ice cream the parlor has at the time we place our order).

Values and *Preferences* include the various types of value that are important to us (e.g., safety, health, money, fun, time, learning and, in the ice cream example, flavor), along with our personal preferences for these types of value and our preferences about risk (e.g., playing football is fun, but the risk of injury is higher than, let's say, the risk of injury in playing golf).

We apply our values and preferences to *consequences* of our decisions. One example of a *consequence* for the ice cream cone decision is eating a chocolate ice cream at the ice cream parlor—a pretty nice consequence as opposed to the consequence of playing football and spraining your ankle.

Why Are Decisions Hard to Make?

There are many skills and behaviors that must come together to make a good decision: understanding and contrasting potentially conflicting preferences and values, dealing with uncertainty and ambiguity, considering significantly different courses of action, and ultimately making a commitment to a choice and taking the necessary steps to fulfilling the commitment. That sounds daunting when you put it all together. No wonder upon reflection many of us consider some of our most important decisions in life were poor decisions that continue to haunt us to this day. Our personal regrets are often the direct consequence of poor decision making.

We're not going to sugar-coat this: Becoming a superior decision maker takes time, persistence and practice. Sure, some of us are naturally better at this than others, but we can all improve. Decision making is an *acquired* skill requiring a step-by-step and repeatable approach.

In fact, you may find what's covered in this book harder to learn than your children, since you are going to have to unravel many poor decision-making habits you probably have fallen into over time. However, by learning the basic principles of a quality decision-making approach and then practicing it with your children, you will quickly find your decision-making ability improving.

What Makes a Quality Decision?

All good decisions, when we look back on them, have the following characteristics:

1. We focused on the right issues that led to the right decision to focus on and then considered significantly different choices associated with that decision.
2. The information we used to make the decision was correct and helped us think about important consequences (both favorable and unfavorable).
3. We understood and considered our personal values and preferences for each of the potential consequences.
4. We compared the choices so that the one we selected was better than any of the others available to us.
5. We committed to the decision we made, and carried it out.

Notice that all of the characteristics about a good decision are about *how* we made the decision, not the consequence of the decision itself. This is a point we will come back to shortly.

Usually, when we have regrets about a decision, or when one of our children makes a poor decision, one or more of the above characteristics are not satisfied. Have you made a "bad" decision lately? A good exercise is to explain why it was poor in terms of the above five characteristics of a good decision.

We also need to make the distinction between good decisions and good outcomes (consequences). A poignant example will make this distinction clear. A few years ago, one of our fathers-in-law had severe blockage of arteries that, if untreated, left him at extremely high risk for a heart attack or stroke. With an over 95 percent success rate, heart bypass surgery was the obvious choice for treatment. Having the procedure done by a highly accomplished, highly recommended surgeon made the decision for treatment even easier. Unfortunately, the father-in-law never made it home from the hospital—he died of complications after the surgery. The decision to pursue the heart bypass surgery was a good one; unfortunately, the consequence was the death of a beloved family member.

A general rule to teach your child early on to lessen the frustration and disappointment that will come at some point in time is that they can't assess the quality of the decision by the consequence *alone* when uncertainty is involved. The best *anyone* can do is to follow an effective decision process for at least that way you will maximize the likelihood of your desired outcome. That's as good as it gets.

When Is It Time to Make a Decision?

Have you ever known a reluctant decision maker—someone who seems to put off making decisions until the last moment or perhaps too late? They always seem to need a little more information or assurance. In general, the longer you wait to make a decision, the fewer the choices you have. A college-bound student who doesn't identify his or her preferred colleges will eventually miss application deadlines and ultimately not attend college, at least for a semester or two.

Just as important is to understand when it is not time to make a decision, when there is value to keeping options open. Have you ever known a "trigger-happy" decision maker—that is, an individual who seems to make decisions too hastily, without sufficient information or consideration, or forgoes valuable downstream options. Children are naturally impatient and impulsive, and not all of them outgrow this behavior.

Clearly, the timing of a decision is a critical concept to understand if we want to be good decision makers. The lesson here is that premature commitment to action limits our search for better information or better alternatives while overly delaying our decisions can make situations worse or problems bigger in the face of fewer choices.

From a psychological perspective, important decisions have an associated degree of anxiety as we enter and exit the intuited "decision window." If you're feeling a sense of anxiety, there is a good chance an important decision is looming. Wouldn't you like to have a solid, proven approach to lean on to get through the decision making?

Creating Good Decision Habits for Life:
A Conversational Approach

In *The Argument Culture: Moving from Debate to Dialogue,*[1] Deborah Tannen describes the overwhelming bias in our culture to debate or argue as our primary means to accomplishment. We approach conversations as a fight between two opposing sides. Rather than listening to our "adversary" during conversation, we are busy formulating our next point to deliver in the debate. Corporations are riddled with this behavioral bias. In this environment decision making boils down to winning debates. The irony is that in these situations decisions are rarely made at all because commitment to a course of action has not been achieved. True commitment is not even a possibility. True commitment is not the objective; winning the debate is.

On the other hand, *structured* conversations designed to create commitment have proven to be a very effective means to making high-quality decisions in organizations. The key word here is *structured*. In the ensuing chapters we will be detailing our *structured*, conversational approach to decision making. But conversations have additional benefits when it comes to learning about decision making.

The best approach we found to introduce decision-making instruction is through the regular conversations you hold with your child. Why use conversations?

We bet that many of you hold regular conversations with your parents, or an old close friend, or your significant other asking their advice and talking through problems and issues that bother you. During these times aren't you at your most attentive, honest, and open to new ideas? A crucial aspect of quality decision making is being open and honest to life's possibilities and alternative courses of action.

Conversations also provide the ideal setting to discuss issues that are bothering your children, or that they are just curious about. As most psychologists point out, one-on-one conversations provide our children with the one thing they often feel they need most but often get least of: *undivided attention from us as parents*. Conversations provide our children with a sense of security, of being wanted, and of trust that few other means in our parenting arsenal can. If you want good decisions, you have to be able to discuss the issues bothering your children.

Further, conversations allow you to demonstrate good decision-making habits without your children seeing you as being a school-teacher. In fact, we urge you to think of yourself more as a helpful coach than a drill sergeant. This book shouldn't be approached like a school course in decision making. Your goal should be to help your children learn how to think about and make decisions, not make the decisions for them. Conversations allow you and your child the freedom to explore various decision alternatives and consequences in a nonthreatening fashion from a learning perspective.

Finally, sometime in the future, the roles will reverse—instead of you coaching and assisting your children in making decisions, they will be helping you. Your nursing home decision will be sooner than you think.

Getting Started

We suggest that you begin by reading the next chapter on the topics of decision equity and decision empowerment and the first three chapters of Part II of the book describing the essence of our FIVE-to-Decide™ conversational approach to decision making. Then, by scanning the end-of-chapter dialogue guides for chapters 6 through 10, you will have a good overview of the FIVE-to-Decide Conversation process steps. This will be a sufficient background for you to begin the process of engaging your child in good-quality decision conversations initiating the pathway to empowering your child to being a good decision maker.

We have tried to break the material down into 15 minute "chunks," since you probably don't have much more time than this to devote at any one time (at least if you're a mother of young children!).

Once you get familiar with the overall approach, we suggest that you then read the book and apply the ideas to a decision that you are interested in making, or one that you recently made that you had some doubts or regrets about. See how the process works, and then go over the parts that might have given you some difficulty. Re-read the end-of-chapter dialogue guides that describe some common problems people have with making decisions, and review how to overcome them. A good approach would be to go through the book with your spouse or partner and work out an example together.

Our experience, based on teaching and working with hundreds of corporate executives, colleagues, friends, and relatives, has been that to teach good decision making you need to focus on real-life decisions. These don't have to be life-altering decisions, but ones that have some relevance to your child in his or her own day-to-day world. Initially, it's best to pick less consequential decisions—e.g., can I have Jill over for a sleepover, or where should the family go for dinner—before you try to tackle decisions that have longer lasting effects.

In the next chapter, we are going to introduce the concepts of decision equity and decision empowerment—the essence of this book.

NOTES

[1] Deborah Tannen, *The Argument Culture: Moving from Debate to Dialogue*, (New York: Ballantine Books, 1999).

From Decision Impoverishment to Empowerment

Have our children's lives become over-scheduled and over-protected? Has our concern, as parents, for our children's futures driven our own behavior to be overly protective to the point that our children have very little opportunity to build their decision-making skills? Rather than empowering our children to becoming good decision makers, are we inadvertently creating a state of *decision impoverishment*?

As parents we often worry about the choices that our children make when they are out of our sight. Who are they playing with and what are they doing? Are they acting responsibly at a friend's party or out driving? Are they being negatively influenced by peer pressure? For instance, studies have shown that the chances of a traffic accident for a 16- or 17-year-old driver are doubled with two peers in the car and quadrupled with three or more present.

Similarly, children themselves are often nervous or anxious about what they should do when placed in unfamiliar or stressful circumstances. Children don't want to do or say things that might embarrass themselves, so they often shy away from opportunities to display their true decision-making capabilities and skills.

The best preparation we can provide our children for coping with these situations is to help them learn how to make good decisions, especially in times of stress, and nurture their sense of responsibility and ownership of the decisions they make. As a child grows in age and experience, we need to increase his or her say in decision making. If we don't, we will find a young adult uncertain and confused as to how to live on their own.

At the same time, we want to be careful not to give a child more autonomy than they can handle. Too much too soon is as bad as too little too late. The key questions for parents are how much say—how much *decision equity*—should a child have and how soon should he or she have it?

Empowered to Make a Decision

When we say that someone is empowered to make a decision, what does it really mean? If you recall from Chapter 1, we said that a decision is a commitment by an individual of something of value, meaning that we can't undo the decision without some cost being incurred. Implicit in this definition are the questions: by whom is this commitment made, do they have the authority to make this commitment, and are they responsible for the outcome and consequences of the decision?

Empowerment therefore means having the authority to decide as well as the responsibility for the outcome and consequences of a decision. However, empowerment has a second part to it. To empower means to equip or supply someone with an ability or capability to do something. Therefore, to *truly* empower someone to make a decision is to mean that we have given them, *first*, the capability to make a decision, and then, *second*, granted the authority and responsibility to make the decision. The two—creating the capability in a child and transferring the authority to a child—are inseparable in principle; but, unfortunately, almost always disconnected in practice. And the biggest culprit of this disconnect, is the absence of any formal training in decision making.

To be empowered to make a decision means having what we call complete decision equity. Decision equity can be thought of as decision ownership and control—who "owns" the decision, including its outcome. Full or 100 percent decision equity—i.e., decision empowerment—means enjoying both the individual freedom and authority to make a decision but also fully accepting the responsibility for the consequences of the decision.

For an individual, anything less than being empowered to make a decision means that at least one other person is involved in the decision in terms of commitment, authority, and responsibility. For parents, determining the appropriate "decision equity share" to be held by your child is something that should be carefully considered. Used judiciously, decision equity can be your child's bridge from decision impoverishment to decision empowerment.

The Gap Between Biological and Societal Milestones in Decision-Making Development

Society itself confers decision empowerment to our children as they grow up. For instance, most states allow teenagers to drive at 16 years of age, join the military or get married at 18, and vote or drink at the age of 21. However, as we now are finding out, these societal guideposts and the biological and psychological aspects involved in decision making don't always quite line up.

Until fairly recently, most scientists thought that the human brain was fully matured by the time a child reached the age of 12. The reason for this belief was that, by the age of 12, a human brain reaches its full physical size and that, by the age of 12, most children's cognitive abilities—meaning the ability to perform formal operations (e.g., reason about logical abstractions or think about the future)—are about the same as an adult.

However, new studies are showing that while the physical growth of the brain stops at the age of 12, internal changes in the brain's physical makeup continue. Furthermore, while a 12-year-old can think about the future impact of a present decision, the reasoning isn't complete. Studies are now showing that a person's brain—and decision-making capability—doesn't fully mature until around the age of 25 in males and around 23 in females. Not until that age can a person make mature, adult decisions and potentially have a complete understanding of the consequences of his or her actions.

In essence, then, we have a built-in "decision maturity gap" between when biology says a person is ready to make a mature decision and what society believes. Therefore, it is even more critical that parents consciously set out to empower their children's decision-making ability by nurturing that ability as well as by transferring authority and responsibility in a harmonized way.

Dividing up Decision Equity

Just as the ownership structure of a business is divided up among equity partners (e.g., Carrie owns 60 percent of the business and Kelly owns 40 percent of the business for a total of 100 percent), so should the *decision equity* (decision ownership) be split between a child and a parent. The more decision equity the child has, the more say and authority the child has in making the decision.

Initially, the split in decision equity between a child and a parent should be decision-specific. That is, for smaller, less consequential decisions a parent may give more decision equity to the child while the parent may reserve much more decision equity for themselves on bigger, more consequential decisions. The concept of decision equity creates a bridge or pathway from having no say or authority in decisions to having complete authority in making decisions, decision empowerment. How a parent and child cross this bridge hand-in-hand is the essence of this book.

A child psychologist friend of ours has written that a child's behavior reflects the progress—or lack of it—towards acquiring cognitive skills and personal power, as well as the integration of the two. Therefore, how much decision equity share you decide on will depend greatly on a child's cognitive skills, which themselves change with age. Additionally, the child's personality and emotional maturity need to also be considered in the equation.

There are five cases for splitting decision equity between a child and a parent. Keep in mind that the amount of decision equity given to a child is *always* dependent on the specific decision. As an example, even the youngest children are usually and should be empowered to make decisions based on simple personal preferences. As an example, choosing a flavor of ice cream to eat is a decision based on simple personal preferences. Consequently, the following discussion on cases for splitting decision equity is intended to provide parents general guidance on decisions that have some consequence.

Case 1: Parent as teacher

In this case, the child is given little or no decision equity. We believe that children as young as 4 years of age can begin to be taught elements of the contents of this book. In fact, at the end of the chapters in Part II of this book you will find exercises you can use to start teaching young children the foundations of good decision making. Therefore, children under four years of age should have little say in making consequential decisions. On the other hand, allowing your child to make choices involving simple personal preferences (e.g., what to eat from a set of choices you create, or color of shirt to wear) is a good way to begin growing their sense of individuality. In this stage of decision-making development, the parent is a teacher.

Case 2: Parent as mentor

In this case, the child or pre-adolescent is given some decision equity, but less than parent's. Preschool children's cognitive skills are adequate to understand and have personal preferences, which are essential building blocks to making decisions. They are at an age where you can start to give them some equity share in the decisions. You might ask them to help make decisions concerning how to spend some family time (e.g., go to the park or visit their cousins), what leisure activity they prefer (e.g., watch television or read a book) as well as what outdoor activities they want to engage in (e.g., play soccer or go swimming).

Around 7 years of age, a child's cognitive skills start to mature quickly. Children now start to think logically about objects and events. At this age a child is able to order and organize the knowledge he or she acquires into differentiated, single structured classes or dimensions, such as weight. However, a child between the ages of 7 to around 11 is not able to reason about the meaning of proportions, correlations, or probability very well. Keep this in mind when you are deciding the level of decision equity you are giving. At this stage of decision-making development, the parent should be working through decisions with their child and so the parent's role is one of being a mentor.

Case 3: Parent as partner

In this case, the adolescent or young adult and parent have equal or approaching equal equity shares. Once a child is around 12, the cognitive skills increase dramatically. Children of this age now start to understand "relations between relations" and are able to look at situations across more than one dimension. While adolescents can start to reason like adults, their brains are undergoing massive changes that are allowing them to improve only slowly the quality of their decision making. The very last part of the brain that matures is called the prefrontal cortex—the part of the brain that controls planning, problem solving, decision making, goal-directed behavior and prioritization, level of attention, and the initiation and execution of deliberate actions. As we noted earlier, this maturation process does not end until about the ages of 23 to 25.

At this stage of decision-making development the parent and child can partner on many decisions, each helping the other to think through the decision-making process. There are still decisions that the parent will retain decision authority on, such as which school the child attends and overall schedule of the child's activities; but at this stage of decision-making development, many decisions should be approached on an equal partner basis. Therefore, the role of the parent is one of being a decision-making partner.

Case 4: Parent as advisor

In this case, the young adult has more decision equity than the parent. As a child becomes a young adult, it is a critical time to increase your child's decision equity closer to full decision empowerment. Remember, decision empowerment is an issue of both capability and the granting of responsibility and authority. So we, as parents, need to make sure our child's decision-making skills are commensurate with the degree of decision equity granted. A young driver is seen by society as fully empowered with respect to decisions and actions on roads and highways. If the adolescent or young adult is not prepared properly, the consequences can be tragic not only to the driver, but his or her family as well as third parties. Consequently, your goal as a parent is to ensure your child is prepared for these new responsibilities and authorities and to ensure that your child is prepared to make good decisions outside of your presence.

At this stage of decision-making development, the parent should still reserve the right to veto any decision that the young adult demonstrates insufficient judgment or consideration for. But this option to veto a decision should be considered only as a last resort since the goal at this stage of decision-making development is to have the parent participate as an advisor, not a judge.

Case 5: Parent as trusted friend and loved one

In this case, the daughter or son is empowered to make decisions. Prepared or not, your daughter or son—barring issues of mental or physical health or incarceration—will be empowered to make decisions for themselves some day. Your goal as a parent, and the ultimate goal of this book, is to prepare them to be truly empowered to make decisions by ensuring they are fully capable of making good decisions. One of the greatest satisfactions, if not greatest relief, for a parent is to witness the maturing of a son or daughter into a fully empowered adult. The satisfaction of knowing your son or daughter is truly prepared for this major milestone in life is immeasurable. At this stage of decision-making maturity, the parent becomes a trusted friend and loved one.

Although the decision-making relationship between the parent and son or daughter changes over time, hopefully there always will be a relationship. And as a parent ages the tables may turn as the son or daughter becomes the advisor, trusted loved one, and friend.

Additional Decision Equity Guidelines

Deciding the proper amount of decision equity for our children, especially adolescents, will be very difficult at times. We know that we authors gave our parents a hard time when they limited what we could do as teenagers, even though in retrospect, they were probably correct to do so. Setting limits is a key to good decision making.

For instance, parents should think through and agree in which decisions children will have no decision equity, such as in the case of drinking or smoking under a certain age. These decisions are part of a class of pre-made decisions that fall under "family policies." You may wish to create a "decision inventory" detailing out which decisions you as parents have 100 percent decision equity and which others you are willing to share.

Further, knowing how your child's cognitive skills change is important in understanding what your child can and cannot reasonably reason about. Do not give them more decision equity than they can handle for their age. It will only serve to frustrate them.

Below are a few guidelines we think parents should keep in mind to help foster your child's decision-making skills and for determining their decision equity as they grow. Since small decisions precede large decisions, the earlier you can start with your child, the better.

A. For younger children, 4 to 7, empowerment concerns decision-making structure and limits:

- First, don't give your child choices you don't intend on letting them make. Not only is this unfair, but it sends a conflicting message that it is the parent's decision versus the child's decision.
- Second, don't provide too many choices. Young children have a hard time dealing with multiple alternatives, leading to doubt and anxiety. They do not have the cognitive skills to differentiate among more than a couple of alternatives.
- Third, hold children accountable for their decisions. A parent shouldn't take away the consequences of a poor decision made or the child won't learn from their mistakes.
- Fourth, ensure that commitments made are commitments completed. Decisions are commitments, i.e., promises to do something. Children need to learn very early that when they make a decision, they need to carry it out.
- Finally, allow decisions to be reversed. If a child recognizes that they made a poor decision, then allow them to reverse it. But such a reversal should not be penalty free, or again the child will not learn.

B. For pre-adolescent children, ages 8 to 11, empowerment focuses more on the decision-making process. In addition to the guidelines above, you should consider:

- First, help the child figure out what is most important in their decision. Proper decision focus and determining what information is "decision relevant" are key to quality decision making.
- Second, review poor decisions. Younger children may not

understand why a decision is a poor one, but at this age they can begin to understand how failure to follow steps in making a decision can lead to a poor decision.

- Third, encourage your child to make decisions. Good decision making is a habit that needs to be created. Work at finding "safe" decisions that your child can make so that they can learn how to make good decisions.

C. For adolescents and young adults, ages 12 to 18, empowerment concerns honing their decision-making skills and increasing the transfer of decision-making authority and responsibilities. In addition to the guidelines above, you should consider:

- First, explain your own decisions. Adolescents will want to understand your thinking behind the decisions you have made.
- Second, offer your own life experiences in decision making, both the good decisions and the bad. Parables have been an effective means to teach throughout time.

Now that we know what is decision making and what is decision empowerment, we can turn our focus on how to empower our children to become good decision makers—the topic of Part II.

FIVE-to-Decide: A Conversational Approach to Decision Empowerment

3

The Five Questions of Decision Making

"Everything should be made as simple as possible, but not simpler."
Albert Einstein (1879–1955)

The essence of good decision making is wrapped up in five questions. If you are making a tough decision or helping someone make a tough decision, each of these questions should be addressed. The intent of this chapter is to take Einstein's genius to heart and to briefly characterize an effective decision-making conversation that is complete, but is *as simple as possible*.

Having a conversation that honestly and thoughtfully answers these five questions covers the essence of this book and will lead to good, defendable decision making. The remainder of this book is devoted to guiding parents and their children to true decision empowerment and decision-making mastery through structured conversations addressing the following five questions.

Question 1: What is the decision and what are the choices?

Before you dive into your choices and possible options for a decision, stop, step back, and answer the first part of the question, "What are we deciding?" What *really is* the decision to decide? Is the decision that needs to be addressed a *bigger or broader* scoping decision than the decision that immediately comes to mind? Or should the decision be more narrowly defined? As an example, is the decision should we buy a new car or repair our current car? Or, which new car should we buy? Or, where should we have the car repaired?

After you are clear on what the decision is, then develop your choices. If the decision is "Should we buy a new car or repair our current car?" the possible choices might include: (1) buy a new car that is $20,000 or less; (2) completely repair the car at the dealer; or, (3) completely repair the car at an independent automotive repair shop.

If you are uncertain about the possible consequences of your decision or would like to have some downstream options for yourself, build those options into your choices. With this in mind for the example, you might want to add an additional choice, (4) partially repair the car at an independent automotive repair shop with the intent of keeping it for no more than six months. The motivation for the fourth choice is to minimize the expense of a repair in order to make the purchase of a new car more affordable over the next several months.

Question 2: Why is the decision tough to make?

Is it obvious which choice is best? If it is obvious, then make the decision and be done with it. If it is not obvious, you must ask yourselves why? Be honest with yourselves here! Why is the decision tough to make? Decisions are tough to make because of difficult value trade-offs (e.g., cost of repair or purchase versus the enjoyment of a new car), uncertainty (e.g., will a partial repair of the car result in another breakdown over the next couple of months?), or not having good choices—back to Question 1.

Answering Question 2 requires pinpointing the issues and concerns that make the decision difficult and understanding the nature of each of the issues and concerns as defined above. For issues or concerns that are uncertainties, can you make a reasonable assumption? If yes, what is the assumption? (e.g., a partial repair of the car *will not* result in another breakdown over the next couple of months or, conversely, a partial repair of the car *will* result in another breakdown over the next couple of months—whichever is more likely). We will be addressing issues that need to be addressed as uncertainties in Chapters 7 and 9.

Question 3: What are the types of value we need to consider?

Building on the answers to Questions 1 and 2, what types of value should be considered in the decision (enjoyment, health, safety, learning, family quality time, charity, pain, money, personal fulfillment, or time)? Consider each choice before you complete the list of types of value that are associated with the decision. For each type of value make sure you understand from whose perspective the value is being considered (e.g., my enjoyment and your money).

Question 4: Which is the best choice and why?

Building on the answers to Questions 1, 2, and 3, which is the best choice and why? Considering each of the choices, the issues and concerns (i.e., value tradeoffs, assumptions, or uncertainties), and the types of value associated with the choices, understand and articulate why one of the choices is best. Attempt using a "devil's advocate" approach to argue why other choices could be best. What is the underlying *value story* for the "best" choice? Why is the best choice superior to the other choices?

In the example, the value story might be: Since we are going to buy a new car over the next six months or so, we will minimize our total cost (including the value of a trade in) by going ahead and buying the new car now. Additionally, by doing this, we will virtually eliminate the concern of having another car breakdown and it sure will be a lot more fun having a new car.

Question 5: Are we ready to make the decision?

There are two cases here:

A. If yes, which choice are we choosing and what is the commitment?

B. If no, what do we need to do in order to make the decision?

Are you ready to commit to a choice and the responsibilities of fulfilling the actions required of that commitment? Are you ready to assume responsibility for the potential consequences of the actions you and others will be taking? Are you clear on what these commitments are? If you answer "yes" to all of these, then you are ready to make the decision. If you answered "no" to any of these questions, then you need to identify what you must do to become decision-ready.

In the example, the commitment might be to go shopping for a new car this weekend with the intent of making the purchase.

Consider this chapter as a quick introduction. Commit these questions to memory. The next time you need to make a decision or are having a conversation with someone about making a tough decision, think about these questions. Notice which of these ques-

Exhibit 3.1

The Five Questions of Decision Making

1. What is the decision and what are the choices?
2. Why is the decision tough to make?
3. What are the types of value we need to consider?
4. What is the best choice and why?
5. Are we ready to make the decision?
5a. If yes, which choice are we choosing and what is the commitment?
5b. If no, what do we need to do in order to make the decision?

tions come naturally to mind for you and which questions you might tend to skip.

Empowering your children to become good decision makers entails teaching your children to think well about these questions. In the remainder of this book, we are offering a conversational approach to guide you, as a parent, in teaching and mentoring your child to decision empowerment.

Now we will delve into FIVE-to-Decide, a conversational approach for making good decisions.

The FIVE-to-Decide Conversation

Ricky: Mom, I'm going to go over to Tony's house for a sleepover party on Saturday! Okay?

Mother: Are we doing anything on Saturday? You better ask Dad!

Ricky: Dad, Mom says I can go to Tony's sleepover party on Saturday; but, that I should check with you to make sure we're not doing anything. We're not, right?

Father: No, we don't have anything special planned. I guess it's alright.

Ricky: Thanks Dad!

Although the parents and the child had an efficient conversation, the parents just missed a great opportunity to sharpen their child's decision-making skills.

In this chapter, we will be introducing the *FIVE-to-Decide Conversation* for decision making and revisit the above conversation.

The FIVE-to-Decide Approach to Decision Making

As we mentioned in Chapter 1, many skills and behaviors must come together to make a good decision: understanding and contrasting potentially conflicting preferences and values, dealing with uncertainty and ambiguity, considering significantly different courses of action, and ultimately making a commitment to a choice and taking the necessary steps to fulfilling the commitment.

We have created the FIVE-to-Decide Conversation with several goals in mind. First, we wanted an approach that young children could learn easily and quickly—such as memorizing something using one hand. We have also created little rhymes and images that will further help your child (and you) remember what to do in each step.

Second, while each of the steps in the FIVE-to-Decide Conversation builds on the previous step, as you will shortly see, you don't need to use all five steps together before getting value from any one of them. For instance, by just training your child to improve the *focus* of his or her decision, he or she will greatly improve the decisions they make. Don't wait to learn the whole process before getting started.

Third, the FIVE-to-Decide Conversation is really a framework for achieving high-quality conversations leading to high-quality decisions. As we discussed earlier, and will discuss more in a few minutes, the best way to teach decision making to children is through holding a series of dialogues that the parent and child can share during each step of the decision process. We have created a flexible and robust decision framework that parents can use to tailor the language and style to match their approach to parenting.

Fourth, a major goal of the FIVE-to-Decide Conversation is to get your children (and you as parents) to start to think about decision making itself. Each step in our approach is designed to get children to visualize the decision process. The more that our children are aware that there is a defined process involved in making a good decision, the more they will be aware of the quality of their thinking and the quality of their decision.

Finally, the end goal of the FIVE-to-Decide Conversation is to have children internalize the decision-making thought process so that it becomes a natural, systematic approach to use as they grow older and throughout their adulthood. The ultimate goal is to build your child's ability to make and be fully responsible for their decisions.

The FIVE-to-Decide Conversation Steps

Let's return to the "sleepover party" conversation and provide a demonstration of how that conversation might unfold applying the FIVE-to-Decide approach. We'll be breaking down each of these steps in subsequent chapters, so consider this just an introductory test drive. This might feel a little cumbersome at first, but after a couple of attempts the process will feel quite natural.

Focus

F

Step 1: The Focus Dialogue

"Look up, look down, then all the way around."

Identifying the right decision to focus on and its associated choices is a key skill and perhaps one of the most important steps in making good decisions. The objective of the *Focus Dialogue* is just that—identify the right decision and its choices. We get started by declaring that a decision needs to be made. This will be a clear signal to the child (or parent) that they should begin the structured conversation.

Ricky: Mom, I'm going to go over to Tony's house for his sleepover party on Saturday! Okay?

Mother: That sounds fun. You know, though, Saturday is the last day your Uncle, Aunt, and Cousin are staying with us. They'll be leaving on Sunday around noon. It looks like we should think this through and make a good decision on this.

Ricky: But I missed Tony's party last year, and I don't want to miss it again.

Mother: I understand that, honey. Let's make sure we do the right thing here since this decision impacts more than just you. Okay?

Ricky: Oh, alright.

Now that the parent and child have established that its time to make a decision, the conversation should be focused on determining what the *real* decision is.

Mother: What do you think the decision is that we need to make?

Ricky: Whether or not I should go to Tony's sleepover party?

Mother: Let's check that.

At this point in the dialogue, do you think that is the *right* decision to focus on? You can find out by following our rhyme of "look up, look down, then all the way around."

"Look up" means consider a related "bigger and broader" decision, such as, what will the family do on Saturday taking into consideration they have visiting relatives. "Look down" means consider a related "smaller and narrower" decision, such as, how should Ricky get to and back from the party? Now, of these three possible decisions, which seems to be the *right* decision to focus on? We are actually deciding on what the decision is—that's the essence of the *Focus Dialogue*.

Mother: What is a bigger and broader decision to whether you should go to the party?

Ricky: I'm not sure.

Mother: How about, what should our family do on Saturday considering it's the last day we have our relatives here?

Ricky: That sounds okay.

Mother: What do you think a smaller and narrower decision is?

Ricky: How should I get to the party?

Mother: That sounds good.

Mother: So, of those three decisions, what is the right decision for us to focus on?

Ricky: What should our family do on Saturday?

Mother: I think you're right!

Now that the right decision has been identified, "then all the way around" means to consider several distinctly different choices for that decision.

Mother: Now we need some good choices for that decision. What do you think the choices are?

Ricky: Well, one choice is I go to Tony's party and you guys do something with Aunt Jean, Uncle Donny, and Cousin Alice.

Mother: Okay. Another choice is for you to go to Tony's party, and we'll pick you up before bedtime so that we can do something with the whole family on Sunday morning.

Ricky: Alright. But don't pick me up too early!

Mother: Right now that's just a consideration. We are not choosing yet. What else could we do?

Ricky: Well, one choice is that I don't go at all to the party and we all do something together on Saturday.

Mother: That's right. We need to consider that possibility too. So we have three different choices to consider. That's our focus.

Step 2: The Information Dialogue

Information

FI

"What makes the decision hard or tough? What information is just enough?"
    If the decision is obvious, you probably have all the information you need to make the decision. However, as our little snippet of dialogue shows, even "simple" decisions can require more thought than at first glance.
    Therefore, a question you need to help your child ask is whether

the decision is hard or tough to make. Answering "Why is the decision hard or tough to make?" uncovers the information needs and issues of value—something we will look at more in the next step. Is there something we can find out prior to making the decision that would make the decision easier to make? For example, let's say there are some special events at the sleepover party, at what time would they conclude?

A second question your child then needs to ask herself or himself is, "Is there anything else I need to know to help make the decision?" Often this question will raise important uncertainties or unknowns, if any, that need to be accounted for.

Mother: What makes this decision hard to make?

Ricky: Well, maybe I should spend my time with the family; but I really want to go to Tony's sleepover party!

Mother: So we need to consider what others want to do and how what you do impacts this. Is there anything else you would like to know to help make the decision?

Ricky: Yes. If I stay with our family on Saturday, what are we going to do?

Mother: I'm not sure. I know your Aunt and Uncle have some packing to do. But I think we should leave it up to them on what it is they would like to do with us on Saturday.

Ricky: That's just great. We might end up doing nothing!

Mother: Well, that's possible.

In summary, the decision is hard because they want to be considerate of their relatives' desires. Additionally, they have some uncertainty since it is not clear on what Saturday's activities would be if the child stays with the extended family for the day.

Value

F I V

Step 3: The Value Dialogue

"What's 'good'? What's 'bad'? Let's ask Mom or Dad."

For each choice, the child and the parent should think about and identify what types of value are relevant and from whose perspective should we be considering those values. Categories or types of value include: enjoyment (fun), health, safety, learning, family quality time, charity, pain, money, personal fulfillment, and time.

Mother: Besides, you, your Dad and me, is there anyone else we should consider for their values or preferences for this decision?

Ricky: Yes. We should consider what Aunt Jean, Uncle Donny, and Cousin Alice want.

Mother: I think you are exactly right.

Ricky: How about Tony? Shouldn't we consider what he thinks?

Mother: I think how your friend, Tony, thinks about this is important. But don't you think we should focus on our family's perspective since it is our family's decision?

Ricky: You're right.

At this point, the mother and the child have established whose values and preferences to consider in making this decision. Now they need to identify the types of values to include in the *Evaluate Dialogue*.

Mother: What types of values are important for this decision? Fun? Safety? Family Quality Time? Health?

Ricky: Seems like fun and family quality time are the only things important here.

Mother: From whose perspective should we be considering fun?

Ricky: Mine!

Mother: Okay. I agree. From whose perspective should we consider family quality time?

Ricky: Our whole family?

Mother: I think so. We should consider all of our family including your Uncle, Aunt, and Cousin.

Ricky: That sounds right.

Mother: Good. I think we're ready to evaluate our choices now.

Evaluate   **Step 4: The Evaluate Dialogue**

FIVE   *"Let's do the math to find the best path."*

The intent of the *Evaluate Dialogue* is to value score each of the choices using the types of value identified in the *Value Dialogue*. Key to this dialogue is to remember that you are scoring the choices from a specific individual's or group's perspective and preferences— not necessarily your own (e.g., *Ricky's* fun and *the extended family's* family quality time).

Mother: Let's score each choice for your fun and our family quality time. Remember our scoring system. For fun, a zero (0) means that the alternative has no value for that type of preference; a one (1) means some value, but no big deal; a two (2) means it is a lot of fun; and a three (3) means it is fun to the extreme. You can think of few things more fun than this.

Making a scorecard on paper greatly helps in completing the *Evaluate Dialogue.*

Mother: Let's start with the first choice: You go to Tony's party and stay overnight for the entire party. How do you score that for your fun?

Ricky: I give that a 2. This sleepover party is going to be a lot of fun.

Mother: I agree. I think it is about a 2 for you too. How would you score going and staying for the entire party on our family quality time?

Ricky: Well, I guess it doesn't score anything since I won't be with family.

Mother: That's right, so we will score that zero.

Mother: Okay. Let's consider the second choice—you go to the party but leave early so that we can do something with your Aunt and Uncle on Sunday morning. How would you score that for fun?

Ricky: That's alright. It'll still be pretty fun. I know it will be crummy leaving early, so it's not as good as staying for the whole party; but it is still something I'd really enjoy. It's better than a 1—no big deal. I'd still give it a 2.

Mother: I understand and agree. I think it is still a 2 for you. How would you score it for our family quality time?

Ricky: I'll be spending some time with Aunt Jean, Uncle Donny, and Cousin Alice and you and Dad. It would be good to be home when they leave. I guess I'd score it a 2.

Mother: I like the way you are thinking about this. Spending the morning with them before they leave would be a good gesture and good family time. So I agree. I think it is a 2.

Mother: So there is one last choice we need to consider and score—you don't go to the party and stay with family on Saturday. How would you score that for your fun?

Ricky: Well, I don't know what we are doing on Saturday if I stay with family. The most I'm scoring that is a 1.

Mother: We'll come up with something fun to do, I promise. I'll talk with Dad, Aunt Jean, Uncle Donny, and Cousin Alice and make sure it's something you will enjoy too. I think it will be better than a 1; but I'll stick with your score of 1.

Mother: We have one last value question. How would you score staying with family all day on Saturday from a family quality-time perspective?

Ricky: It's good but it's not a 3. I'd give it a 2.

Mother: Yes, I think it is a 2 for family quality time.

Although this dialogue might seem on first pass a little compli-cated, it isn't. Our experience is that children learn quickly to apply the simple zero through three scoring rules (we will introduce neg-ative scores as well in Chapter 9) and often will eagerly debate you on your scores!

Mother: Let's add up the scores and see how the three choices compare. For the first choice—you go and stay for the entire party—we have a 2 for your fun and a zero for family quality time for a total of 2 points.

For the second choice—you go to the party but leave early to spend time with family—we have a 2 for your fun and a 2 for family quality time for a total of 4 points.

And, for the third choice—not going to the party at all and staying with family for the entire day—we have a 1 for your fun and a 2 for family quality time for a total of 3 points.

Ricky: Yes. I could see where this was heading. But, it sounds all right to me.

Mother: Based on our evaluation, going to the party but not stay-ing overnight sounds like the best choice. Does that sound right?

Ricky: It does.

Mother: It seems like a good compromise.

Decide   ## Step 5: The Decide Dialogue

"Choose the best thing to do, and keep the promise true."

Up to this point, Ricky and his mother have had a good conver-sation, but they haven't *made* the decision. They haven't *made* a commitment to a choice. The objective of the *Decide Dialogue* is to make the commitment to a choice and all the responsibilities asso-ciated with making that commitment.

Mother: Are we ready to decide? Are we ready to make a commitment?

Ricky: I am.

Mother: What is our decision?

Ricky: Our decision is that I go to the party but not stay for the sleepover, so that I can spend time with our family on Sunday morning before Aunt and Uncle leave.

Mother: I think so. That's our commitment. You did a great job thinking this through with me. I'll talk to Dad, Aunt Jean, and Uncle Donny about what we can do on Sunday morning that we would all enjoy. Maybe we'll all go out for breakfast. How does that sound?

Ricky: All right!

In the following chapters, you will find detailed discussions about how to have each of the five dialogues illustrated in this chapter. Keep in mind that each of these dialogues can and should be tailored to fit your parental style and beliefs. Our goal is to provide you, as a parent, with all of the coaching and tools you will need. Some parents will incorporate nearly everything this book has to offer. Other parents will focus more on the principles in the book and customize the five dialogues along the lines of the "The Five Questions in Decision Making" presented in Chapter 3. Use your intuition to make this right for you and your child. Empowering your child to be a good decision maker is one of the greatest gifts you can give your child. The following chapters will tell you how.

5

Creating a Satisfying Conversation

Thinking back as a child, with whom did you have the most satisfying conversations? Your best friend? Maybe a close cousin you used to hang around with? Your parents? One of the authors relates that his best conversations growing up were with his grandfather.

> I can still see my grandfather sitting in our big chair in the living room, smoking his favorite cigar and sipping his scotch whiskey. Whenever he was visiting and I happened to be facing a difficult situation, I would ask my grandfather for his advice. As I talked, grandfather would take everything in, frown a bit for a moment or two, and then start to ask simple, but to me seemingly amazingly difficult to answer, questions. Through his Socratic-like questioning, my grandfather would lead me to understand first that what I was experiencing wasn't unique, and second, that if I thought a bit more about the situation, I could reason out a pretty good solution to whatever problem of the day I was facing.

For one of the authors, as he looks back at it now as an adult, it was his grandfather's patient and intense listening, genteel questioning, and nonjudgmental attitude that made him seek out his grandfather for advice. His grandfather never imposed himself into the conversation nor said, "I think this is the way you should do it."

We think that most satisfying conversations are like this: talking to someone who cares and who listens patiently to our problems and then helps us think our way to a solution.

Making the Most of FIVE-to-Decide

As can be seen from the conversation in the previous chapter, your role is to help your child articulate what the decision is and to understand the choices that are open to him or her through a series of dialogues with your child. Note that you do not do the thinking for them, but act as a mentor guiding them through the steps that will lead to a high-quality decision.

Many opportunities arise every day for holding decision-focused conversations with your children, probably more than you are aware. We are constantly holding conversations that can help teach decision making all the time—at dinner, in the car, playing with them, or reading to them. Bedtime stories are very useful in teaching decision making to young children.

One of the author's children is four years old, and she loves to have stories read to her. During these stories, her father gently questions his daughter as to what the characters in the story are trying to do and why. He asks what would happen if the characters acted in a different way and what might cause them to decide to go that way. This approach works well not only with familiar stories, but especially so with new ones where his daughter has to guess what characters are going to do next.

Sometimes asking your son or daughter to make a choice is also a way to start a conversation. For example, where should we go out to eat dinner with grandma and grandpa? We are not advocating that you turn every conversation associated with making a decision into a lesson in decision making. Your children will stop talking to you. However, as you will quickly discover, there will be many learning opportunities to sharpen your child's skills.

There may also be times when you need to be proactive in starting a FIVE-to-Decide conversation. For instance, when you see the usual signals that something is bothering your son or daughter, you should gently nudge them into a FIVE-to-Decide conversation. Unusual nervousness, agitation, anxiety, asking a lot of seemingly irrelevant questions, or becoming very quiet are often indications that an important decision needs to be made. FIVE-to-Decide will provide you with a new approach to start these important conversations and resolve important issues with your child.

On the other side, when you feel your child is procrastinating on an important decision or has just plain forgotten about an upcoming important decision, the approach will be a simple but obvious attempt by you to inspire your child to rise to the decision-making occasion.

Elements of a Good Conversation

In teaching children decision making, we think that you should strive to hold one-on-one conversations with each of your children separately. Learning decision making is not really a team sport, and trying to teach several children at once, although fun, may not be as productive as a one-on-one approach. There may be times when there is a "family decision" that needs to be made—where should we go on vacation—that you can use as a teaching moment, but generally one-on-one is best.

Additionally, you will want to tailor the process to the age of each of your children. A teenager is more adapt at being able to express fully all the choices involved in a decision than an 8- or 9-year-old. Moreover, the Evaluate Dialogue scoring system must be tailored to match your child's ability to work with numbers. We will discuss this in Chapter 9.

Most important is to remember that you are having a *conversation* with your child, not a *monologue*. Certain rules of good conversation should be followed to gain the most out of the learning process as discussed in Exhibit 5.1. As we will indicate in each of the following chapters, disregarding these rules are often the reason why you may find the FIVE-to-Decide Conversation not working. Respecting your child and his or her opinions is the most important rule to remember.

And there is one final but important point about using conversations for decision making. Through years of corporate experience, it has become evident that making high-quality decisions with groups or teams requires a structured conversation. The principles of the FIVE-to-Decide conversation are grounded in this understanding of effective corporate decision making. The concepts of this book can be easily translated into approaches for effective team decision making. This is the topic of a forthcoming book.

Decision Habits

Since few of us have ever been formally trained in making decisions, we most likely have developed some poor decision habits. These habits are a creation of our temperament, personality, and experience and are often very hard to overcome.

Furthermore, we often pass these decision habits unknowingly on to our children. If we are in the habit of making hasty decisions, our children are prone to learning that habit as well. Of course, our children's temperament and individual character also greatly

Exhibit 5.1

Rules for Good Conversations

Rule 1: Listen attentively to your child. As parents, we sometimes fall into the trap of talking to our children instead of really listening to what they are saying. Nothing can deflate a child's interest in learning faster than not paying complete attention to them. Children crave having the full, one-on-one attention of their parents. Make this time special for them.

Rule 2: Don't interrupt your child. If you look at the conversation at the beginning of the chapter, you'll see that the mother does not interrupt the child, but lets him fully explain his understanding of the issue. It is tempting to jump in and help but then you become the decision maker, not the child.

Rule 3: Don't criticize your child in front of the family about their ability to learn the *FIVE-to-Decide* approach or make a decision. What this means is that you should not be critical of your son or daughter for not making what you see to be the correct decision. Especially avoid making sarcastic remarks or ridiculing your child. Instead, you should be praising the child for what he or she is doing correctly, and only correct specific mistakes.

Rule 4: Don't talk down to your child. Remember what we call the "child's eye"—the world from your son or daughter's point of view. Always remember that the decision is being taken from the child's perspective, not yours. There are things that you perceive as an adult—both because you can reason better as well as your own experience—that your son or daughter does not yet understand. Do not ask or expect the child to see the world as you do.

Rule 5: Take your time. Don't rush making a decision. Doing so will only reinforce bad habits. We all know what happens when we rush.

Rule 6: Avoid using the *FIVE-to-Decide* approach to advocate a particular choice. It is sometimes tempting for a child (or parent) to "work backwards," using the approach to justify or rationalize a decision he or she has already made.

Rule 7: Don't allow your child to consider an alternative if that alternative is not truly available. It is unfair and discouraging to pretend your child has a choice when you won't (for whatever reason) let them make it.

Rule 8: Respect your son or daughter's opinions. Remember, your child is the important person in the conversation, not you.

influence how they make decisions, but don't underestimate your influence.

To help illustrate these habits, as well as demonstrate what we think are good decision behaviors, we have created a small ensemble of characters, which we call the *Little Decision Makers™*, that we will refer to in different parts of the book. We will use these characters as "reminders" to both you and your child as to what you may want to watch out for in the FIVE-to-Decide Conversation—both good and bad. We have found out that for young children especially, having characters to help them understand the decision process is more effective than just trying to explain it to them.

For instance, one of the Little Decision Makers is named "Skip the Quick." Skip is a bright boy, but is very impatient. He always wants to act first and then decide later. He skips over important steps in the decision process, which leaves him with few choices. His favorite expressions are "It is easier to just do . . ." or "All we have to do is . . ." or "Why don't we just do . . ." Does Skip the Quick remind you of anyone you know—maybe yourself? Although as a rule we don't like labeling people, if you see your son or daughter making a hasty decision, a gentle reminder such as "Let's not be a Skip the Quick here" can help them slow down.

Claire Smart-Choice is a sixteen year old who has mastered the concepts and approaches in this book. She is the "big sister" to the rest of the gang introduced below and she provides guidance and support to the other characters. Claire's favorite expression is "You need to follow the decision process!" Chapter 11 is devoted to her summary of the FIVE-to-Decide Conversation and throughout the book she offers simple summaries of concepts and approaches. Look for her picture in the margins of the pages for her comments.

There are five other children and adolescents who make up our Little Decision Makers cast (see the sidebar on page 39). Of course, each character exaggerates one particular decision-making characteristic to make a point. In reality, all of us at one point or another have exhibited them. Do any of the decision-making biases reflected in our cast members sound familiar to you?

Throughout the book you will see the "Don't" symbol in the margin as warnings of where their biases can creep into your thinking and reduce the quality of your decision making.

While we haven't shown them, lurking just out of view is another set of characters—our Little Decision Makers' parents. They include Browbeater Bill, Anne the Advocate, Dave the Decider, and Paul and Pauline Patience. You can probably guess how they make decisions, and how they interact with and influence their children's decision making.

If you find yourself getting frustrated with the FIVE-to-Decide Conversation—say, you find yourself moving from Paul or Pauline Patience to Anne the Advocate or Dave the Decider because your child just can't seem to make a decision—postpone the conversation for a few hours and come back to it. Patience is a major parental virtue in teaching decision making.

Difficulties in Getting Your Child to Learn FIVE-to-Decide

As we mentioned above, you can expect your child (and possibly yourself) to become occasionally frustrated when they follow the *FIVE-to-Decide* approach. The number of steps at first will look formidable, the amount of information you need to consider looks like a lot, the whole process appears time consuming. Once you get going, and hold a couple of conversations, it should become easier and not take that much time. You'll be surprised how natural this will become after a few tries.

As we have indicated, expect your child to get frustrated and possibly angry when they follow the process but the consequence of their decision isn't what they expected. Children, including most teenagers, don't have sufficient experience to understand the complexity of the world they live in, nor abstract ideas like chance, luck, or probability. Bad consequences can arise even for good decisions.

Remember, you will also need to tailor the process—and both you and your child's expectations—based on your children's ages

Alan the Analyzer:
• Over analyzes, over complicates
• Prefers to continue analyzing rather than make a decision
• Favorite Expression: "I have one more possibility to analyze!"

Debra Detail:
• Gets lost in details
• Always wants more information
• Favorite Expression: "I need to know one more thing before I can make the decision!"

Frieda Fun Loving:
• Over emphasizes having fun and undervalues everything else
• Always focuses on the near-term and gives little consideration for the future
• Favorite Expression: "You know, girls just want to have fun!"

Skip the Quick:
• Impatient, jumps to conclusions
• Makes decisions too quickly
• Makes bad assumptions
• Favorite Expression: "It's easy, just do . . . !"

Timothy Timid:
• Doesn't voice his own opinion
• Avoids conflict
• Goes along with what others think and do
• Favorite Expression: "I don't know, what do you think?"

and cognitive abilities. Child psychologists tell us that most children below the ages of 5 cannot distinguish between right and wrong. Additionally, it isn't until a child reaches the ages of 8 to 11 that he or she can start reasoning logically about abstract ideas, and is able to mentally compare and contrast two competing abstract ideas. Furthermore, it isn't until a child is 13 to 15 years old that they begin to think and reason more like adults, and it is not until they reach the ages of 18 to 24 that children become fully able to reason like an adult and consequently be prepared for full decision equity, decision empowerment for all of their decisions. Even at these latter ages, few young adults have the experience of adults to draw upon. Teenagers also present other challenges, such as a pre-disposition to take on risky behaviors.

So, please, don't expect too much from your child too soon. Also, build up your reservoir of patience—remember you will be teaching yourself as well as your child in some cases. Keep the decision process simple until your child can start to understand each of the steps of the FIVE-to-Decide approach. You will know that your child is mastering the process when they can tell you not only what each step is, but also why it needs to be performed. For most kids, don't expect this level of sophistication much before the age of 11 or 12.

In the next chapter, we will begin our FIVE-to-Decide Conversation in earnest with a look at how to create the decision focus.

6

The Focus Dialogue: "Look up, look down, then all the way around."

> *Wife:* What should we do about that big stain on the carpeting in the dining room?
>
> *Husband:* Did you try that carpet stain remover I bought last week? That should get it out.
>
> *Wife:* I did. I think it actually looks worse since I used it.
>
> *Husband:* Well, we'll have to replace the carpeting in the dining room and the living room then.
>
> *Wife:* It's more than that. We'll have to replace all of the carpeting throughout the house or it won't look right.
>
> *Husband:* Well if you want to do that, I think we should remodel the upstairs bathrooms first and replace the carpeting after the bathrooms are remodeled. Otherwise the new carpeting will get all torn up during the remodel.
>
> *Wife:* You know, I was looking at the new homes they're building up in the hills with some real nice views. Maybe we shouldn't do anything to this house and move into one of those new homes.

Does this sound familiar? How many different decisions are discussed in that brief exchange? We count at least four significantly different decisions each with their own set of choices. What is the right decision for this husband and wife to focus on? What to do about the stain in the carpet? Or should it be about deciding to re-model and re-carpet the entire house? It's not very clear, is it? This chapter is about *"deciding about what to decide"*—the Focus Dialogue.

> **Claire's Comment:**
> The Focus Dialogue is about creating a set of smart and different choices for your decision. The *must-learn* concept of this chapter is how to identify the specific decision to focus on. This will take practice to get good at. But you quickly will see how much this will help and change how you make decisions.

Deciding About What to Decide

As we discussed in the previous chapter, identifying the right decision to focus on along with its choices is a key skill and perhaps one of the most important steps in making good decisions. It is also perhaps the most difficult for a parent as well as a child to master.

To get to the proper decision focus, we need to keep in mind exactly what a decision *is*. As stated in previous chapters, a decision is, simply, a commitment of something of value (e.g., our time, money, reputation) that is scarce. A decision also implies that it is not complete until it is acted upon. In business, that action may be the signature on a contract or a handshake on the commitment to fund a project. For a child, the act of commitment may be the exchange of money for an ice cream cone or the commitment to a friend to meet after school in the library to study together. The decision is the act of commitment of something that the individual perceives as having value. The implication is that it costs something of value to unmake a decision.

Ultimately, creating a decision focus is deciding on what we are deciding about. The decision focus is *the set of choices* you will ultimately choose from at the conclusion of the FIVE-to-Decide conversation. Moreover, it should become evident during the Focus Dialogue why we need to make a decision, what or who is driving us to make a decision, and why is it that we need to make the decision right now.

We make dozens of routine decisions every day without really giving much thought as to why we make them. Most of the time this is just fine, but that habit carries over to nonroutine decisions, and that can lead to regrettable consequences that can be avoided through good, solid decision making.

Change—either change we initiate, or change initiated by others or change driven by us having to react to events—drives all decisions. If nothing ever changed, we would never have to make a decision, which sometimes sounds like paradise when the kids are acting up as you try to figure out how to clean the house, take a business call, cook dinner for the in-laws and look presentable, all in the next three hours. Decisions too, then, are closely linked to problem-solving. Being able to focus on the right problem not only means better solutions but also less time wasted on solving the wrong problem. Being good at decision making is a skill needed for good problem-solving.

The Decision Ladder

At any point in time each of us has a multitude of decisions we can consider and act on. These range from being *higher-order* (bigger and broader) decisions, such as should I change my job, on down to *lower-order* (smaller and narrower) decisions, such as should I eat dinner out, or stay home, or skip dinner and exercise tonight. If we took the time to write down all of the potential decisions we could address and act on over, say, the next month, these decisions would roughly fall into a hierarchy of decisions. The biggest and broadest decisions would be at the top of this hierarchy and smaller, narrower decisions would be somewhere down around the bottom.

You can see this by envisioning a ladder, where every rung represents a decision that you could focus on and decide in the near-term, as Exhibit 6.1 shows. Just as you step up the rungs of a ladder, resulting in a broader view of your surroundings, stepping

Exhibit 6.1: Graphical Overview of the Focus Dialogue

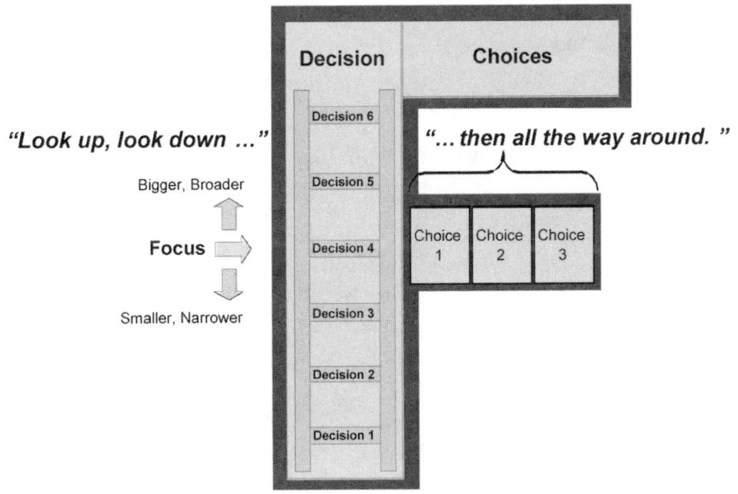

up the rungs of the decision ladder elevates you to bigger and broader decisions. The first part of the Focus Dialogue is all about identifying which rung you are going to focus on for making a decision. The second part will be defining the set of choices that are available—i.e., the decision focus.

The conversation between the husband and wife suggests that the top rung of their decision ladder could be the decision to buy a new home or not. The bottom rung of their decision ladder could be the decision on how to repair the stain on the dining room carpet. A rung somewhere in between could be the decision(s) on what else to fix in the home and the sequence of these fixes.

Defining the Correct Decision Focus

"Look up, look down, then all the way around."

Denise: Mom, I think I want to join an after school intramural soccer team.

Mother: That's wonderful, dear. I didn't know you liked soccer that much. What does it involve?

Denise: Practice is every day after school from 2:30 to 4:30 PM. We have games once a week on Saturday mornings.

Mother: Isn't that going to be a lot of time? Catching the late bus home from school means you won't get home before 5:30 PM. You know your grades have been slipping a little lately, and you need to study more.

Denise: I really want to do this, Mom. I'll cut back on watching TV during the week, and I'll spend extra time every weekend on homework and studying. I promise.

Mother: But aren't you supposed to babysit every Saturday night at the Campbell's?

Denise: Yes, but I'll still have plenty of time after the games to study before I have to go to their house. And I still have all day Sunday to study.

Mother: It also means that I will have to or your Father is going to have to drive you to the games on Saturdays.

Denise: I know I can get a ride with Cindy's Mom.

Mother: Oh, Cindy is going out for the team, too?

Denise: Yes. She said it would be a lot of fun.

Mother: Hmm, this is starting to get complicated. Let's talk more about this with your Father.

There are many possible points for starting the decision conversation in the exchange above. A good start is to declare it's time to think about making a decision. To define the correct focus of a decision, we want to create first a "test case" decision, in other words, an initial decision that we can use to see whether we are considering all the things we need to before we actually embark on making a decision. This boils down to defining the rung on the decision ladder where we begin the Focus Dialogue.

We start by stating this potential decision as a question, typically by using a statement made by the child as a starting point. We do this because a question helps clarify to the child that we are starting down the decision-making path and a question is a natural way to establish the decision-making context. Trust your intuition here. Keep in mind that this is only a "test case" to get the discussion started. In the above dialogue, Denise's initial statement about wanting to join a soccer team turns into the question, "Should I join a soccer team?"

As a simple test to see if Denise is on the right track, ask whether this question meets the criteria for a decision. It certainly appears to, since there is a commitment of something of value—free time—that seems to be scarce. Good start.

Look Up

Now, let's ask ourselves whether the question "Should I join a soccer team" is the right question, or whether there is a better, more appropriate question to focus on. To help find out, we need to, as we like to say, *look up* to the "next bigger and broader" decision. What does the "next bigger and broader" decision mean? What does it mean to be a higher-order decision?

A decision is a higher-order decision in relation to another decision if: (1) it provides additional choices; or (2) it provides completely new and different choices that have broader impact or consequences than the original set of choices. A higher-order decision typically is associated with a higher degree of commitment. The decision to buy a new home or not is a higher-order decision than the decision on how to fix the stained carpet because it provides a completely new and different set of choices that have a broader impact—more money, for one! The decision on *what* should be fixed in the home first is a higher-order decision than the decision on *how* to fix the stained carpet because it provides additional choices.

No matter where you start on your decision ladder, there usually exists a "bigger and broader" decision associated with your "test case." Similarly, there usually is a "smaller and narrower" decision associated with your "test case." "Look up" implies identifying the next "bigger and broader" decision— a higher order decision—right above your "test case" on your decision ladder.

What we want to accomplish is to determine, by moving up a rung from our initial "test case" decision, whether there is some other question (or questions) that really is more appropriate at this point in time than the initial one.

> *Claire's Comment:*
> To help think about a bigger and broader decision, I consider adding one or more "w" questions like "who," "what," "where," or "when" questions. "How" is another good question word in thinking about a bigger and broader decision.

Remember, in Chapter 4, we started out with an initial decision concerning Ricky going to a sleepover. The next bigger and broader decision was what the family should do on Saturday. In the soccer conversation above, what is the next bigger and broader decision with respect to the test decision: "Should I join a soccer team?"

One possibility is, "How should I (the child) spend my free time?" Notice that it wasn't, "Should I try out for soccer or spend my time studying?" These choices are associated with the next bigger decision. Other choices of such a "free time" decision might include babysit more, watch more television, etc., that the child may want to consider. It will take a bit of practice, but your child needs to distinguish between choices and decisions.

Another way to determine the "next bigger and broader" decision is to look at what we might have to forego to make the decision. For instance, if Denise wants to play soccer, then she again reduces her potential study time, playing with other friends, watching TV, etc. These are alternatives other than playing soccer. What they all have in common is the question, "How should I spend my time?" This is a higher-order decision because it provides additional alternatives to choose from.

Identifying a "bigger and broader" decision doesn't mean it is a more appropriate decision to focus on! We'll determine that later. In fact, in many cases you'll identify the next "bigger and broader" decision and quickly conclude that there is no compelling reason to go to this level.

Now, there may not always be a natural "next bigger and broader" decision. For example, in one family the authors know, the children must participate in one after-school activity every semester as a way to broaden the children's horizons. The decision at the beginning of each semester is what school activity each child will participate in, not whether an activity such as soccer will be selected. In regard to some decisions, you as the parent may wish to limit the rungs of the decision ladder your children may climb, just as you do on a real ladder.

Look Down

Once we have defined the "next bigger and broader" decision, we want to "look down" at the "next smaller and narrower" decision. What does the "next smaller and narrower" decision mean? What does it mean to be a lower-order decision?

A decision is a lower-order decision in relation to another decision if: (1) it provides fewer choices; or (2) it provides completely new and different choices that have less impact than the original set of choices. A lower-order decision is usually associated with a lower degree of commitment.

With respect to "Should I join a soccer team?" what is a lower-order decision? In this case, the test decision is already very narrowly defined with the choices of "Yes, commit to an after school intramural team" or "No, don't commit to a team." Therefore, the only way to establish a lower-order decision is to determine if there is a meaningful, related decision with different, less consequential choices. We need to create a lower degree of commitment.

Hmm, that's a little tough. How about the decision, "Should I participate on an after school intramural soccer team for a couple of weeks to see if I like it and can handle the additional schedule load?" We have recast the decision to have less consequential choices by creating a reexamination of the decision two weeks downstream. In business this is analogous to creating an "option."

DON'T! Don't be discouraged if you find this a little tough. Creating the right focus is a skill that requires practice and experience. The more you do it, the easier and more natural it will become. Companies pay business consultants top dollars to help executives of corporations ask the right questions.

> *Don't be like Skip the Quick:*
> • What short cuts might Skip the Quick try to take here?
> • How would you help Skip keep on track?
> • Is there a little Skip the Quick in you or your child?

Once we have stated the next bigger and broader decision and the next smaller and narrower decision, the mother and child have three potential decision perspectives to choose from. The best perspective is the one the mother and child mutually agree to. There are no set rules here. The power of the exercise is to get you to contemplate the different decision perspectives to enable the identification of choices. Remember, the decision focus *is* the set of choices. The act of considering different decision perspectives is only to help generate good, creative choices. The ability to identify creative choices in life is a skill we can all use. In our example, the better of the three decision perspectives seems to be, "How should I spend my free time?" In fact, we might sharpen the question a bit to say, "How should I *best* spend my free time?" since they are going to have to decide among some competing choices.

Why, you ask, couldn't the mother and Denise have selected the question, "Should I join the soccer team?" They could have. It is an acceptable perspective, but it tends to make playing soccer the focal point of the decision rather than having soccer being one of many competing alternatives to choose from. The issue is the value of the time being spent (remember, it is a scarce resource) that is critical, and whether soccer or something else is a better use of that time.

Getting to Choices—the Decision's Focus

Then All the Way Around

The phrase "Then all the way around" suggests that once you have decided on the decision to focus on, you need to consider the significantly different choices you have for the decision. In our example, what different choices exist for "How should I best spend my time?"

First, we want Denise to think of all the other different activities that are possible in the time that would be devoted to soccer in addition to playing soccer. Well, there is studying, going shopping, helping Mom with the house, watching TV, or maybe doing more babysitting, and so on.

Then we want Denise to think about what possible choices there may be among these different activities. For example, Denise could, as she wants, play soccer, then stay up with her studies by not watching television during the week and spending free time on every Saturday and Sunday. Alternatively, she could instead devote more of her time to studying each day instead of playing soccer, giving her free time on Saturday and Sunday to do something else.

On the other hand, Denise could just keep doing her normal activities as before. The point is to identify distinctly different, complete choices from which the child can later select. *These three choices are the focus of the decision.*

This is the most creative step in the entire FIVE-to-Decide process. Take the time to think broadly here. Tap the thoughts and discussion

> Don't be like Timothy Timid:
> • How would you help Timothy open up and voice his thoughts on choices?
> • How would you help Timothy think creatively about different choices?
> • Is there a little Timothy Timid in you or your child?

generated in the first part of this dialogue on defining the decisions and the "right rung" on the decision ladder.

Tom's Birthday Party Decision—The Focus Dialogue

Tom: Dad, I know what I want to do for my birthday party this Saturday.

Father: Oh yeah. And what is that?

Tom: I want to have a party at the park. I've got some great stuff I want to do with my friends.

Father: We better hurry up and decide on what we're going to do. If you want to go to the park this Saturday, we'll need to reserve some tables. And you know, I think they talked about it possibly raining this weekend. We need to make a decision on this.

Tom: I've made my decision. I want to go to the park for my birthday party.

Father: Let's stop and think this through first. Let's talk about this decision. Let's get the Focus right. What do you think is the decision we need to make?

Tom: What should we do if it rains at the park?

Father: That's a good start. What do we do in the Focus dialogue?

Tom: Look up, look down, then all the way around.

Father: That's right. Look up means, consider a related *bigger* and *broader* decision. What do you think is the *bigger* decision?

Tom: Where should my birthday party be?

Father: Nice job! I'm going to add another "w" question to make it a little broader. How about, where should your birthday party be and when?

Tom: I want it on Saturday.

Father: Because of the possibility of rain, I think we should consider the day of the party too. We haven't *decided yet on what we are going to decide*. We're just creating a few different perspectives before we get focused on your choices.

Tom: Okay, I know the routine. So that will be our *bigger and broader* case.

Father: Look down means, consider what might be a related *smaller and narrower* decision. What do you think is the *smaller* decision?

Tom: I really want to have my party on Saturday, so I think the *narrower* decision is where should I have my party on Saturday?

Father: That works. So we have three different ways to think about your birthday party: (1) What should we do if it rains at the park?; (2) Where should your party be and when?; or, (3) Where should your party be on Saturday? Is there any other way to think about this that would be a better perspective?

Tom: No. I think that covers it. (See Exhibit 6.2a.)

Father: What do you think is the best way to think about the decision?

Tom: Where should my birthday party be on Saturday?

Father: Okay. That works for me. That is what we will focus on. (See Exhibit 6.2b.)

Father: 'Then all the way around' means we need to consider the distinctly different choices that we can choose from for this decision. What do you think the choices are?

Tom: One choice is to have the party in the park.

Father: Yes, that is one alternative. But if it rains, you and your friends are going to be pretty disappointed. To make that a good choice, we need some kind of back up plan in case it rains. What do you think?

Tom: Well, I was thinking about going to the arcade with my friends and having some laser tag sessions; but I think we'd have a better time at the park.

Father: Alright, we could use the arcade as a back up plan. So tell me one good alternative.

Tom: We go to the park and if it rains or the weather is bad we dump the park idea and go to the arcade for laser tag.

Father: Perfect. That's one choice. What is another choice you would consider?

Tom: Just go to the arcade for laser tag. That way we don't have to worry about the rain.

Father: I think you're on to this. That's a good alternative too. Any other possibilities you would consider?

Tom: Sure! I can think of other things; but none you'd be willing to pay for!

Father: You got that right. Okay. We have our two choices. (See Exhibit 6.2c.)

Father: One last check. Are we on track here? Do the choices feel right? Are we focusing on the right decision?

Tom: I think so. This feels right to me. And I like the choices.

Father: Me too. I think we have a good *Focus*.

Exhibit 6.2a: Potential Decision Perspectives for Tom's Birthday
Party Decision

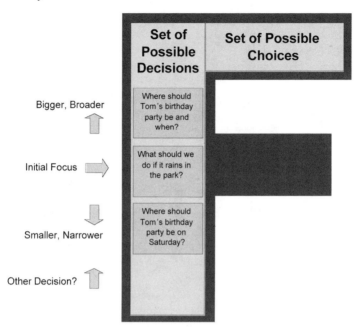

Exhibit 6.2b: Tom's Chosen Decision Perspective for His Birthday
Party Decision

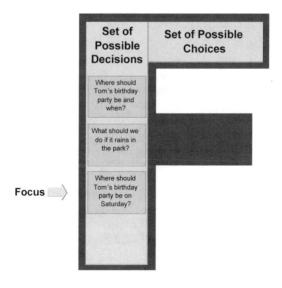

Exhibit 6.2c: The Decision Focus for Tom's Birthday Party Decision

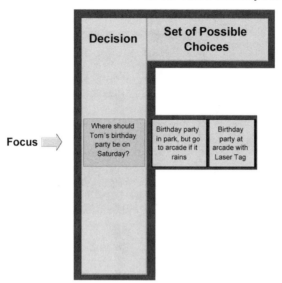

Getting Started

At this point, you've probably realized that this first step—establishing the right focus of the decision—is critical to becoming a good decision maker. Chances are the notion of taking time to *"decide on what you are going to decide"* is a new thought. Just practicing this first step without applying the remainder of the topics in this book (which we *don't* recommend) will improve your decision making immediately.

For yourself, next time you are making a decision, see if you can create the three decision perspectives: (1) the test decision; (2) a "bigger and broader" decision; and (3) a "smaller and narrower" decision. Don't worry if you get stuck on either the bigger or the smaller decision. Just the fact that you are considering the definition of the decision you are contemplating is the key to success here.

For your child, start with some decisions where the three decision perspectives are obvious, at least for you, so that you can be a confident teacher for your child as you attempt to introduce the notion of the decision focus. It is important that you and your child are successful in your early attempts so that you are both motivated to go forward with rest of the FIVE-to-Decide conversation.

We have included some exercises at the end of the chapter to use with children of different ages. These exercises aim to help you understand what you can accomplish and what to expect in regards to your child's decision-making capability. For instance, for very young children, ages 4 to 7, you want to get them to identify what choices they have. For young children, ages 8 to 11, you want to get them to identify bigger and smaller decisions. For the young adolescent pre-teen and young teenager, ages 12 to 15, you want them to realize more about the motivations behind their decision making, such as personal motivations or peer pressure. For teenagers and young adults, ages 16 and older, you want them to realize the potentially long–lasting consequences of their decisions.

The characters introduced at the end of Chapter 5 (Claire Smart-Choice, Alan the Analyzer, Debra Detail, Frieda Fun Loving, Skip the Quick, and Timothy Timid) can be very useful in explaining concerns you may have with your child's initial attempts at the Focus Dialogue and subsequent dialogues discussed in the following chapters. Statements like, "Remember Skip the Quick? He is always trying to take short cuts and jump to conclusions. Let's not be like that. Let's do what Claire says and 'follow the process.'" By using the characters in your explanation, we hope to create a more vivid image for your child, making your guidance easier to remember and more available.

Focus Dialogue Summary

The Focus Dialogue represents the initial critical thinking about a decision that is typically not done—*deciding about what to decide*. Too often we jump ahead to answers, solutions, and decisions before we really have a good handle on the issues, concerns, and questions that need to be dealt with. Getting to the list of choices associated with the right decision at this point in time is the ultimate goal of the Focus Dialogue. And that is a handful! But to become a good decision maker you must master this step.

A high-quality Focus Dialogue accomplishes three goals:

1. Considers different decisions—from broader and bigger to narrower and smaller—before agreeing on the specific decision to pursue;

2. Results in significantly different, compelling, and complete choices;

3. Feels intuitively right for both child and parent.

If your Focus Dialogue accomplishes these, you are ready to move on to the Information Dialogue.

Exercises

For very young children ages 4 to 7:

1. Introduce the terms "decision" and "choice" to your child's vocabulary.

2. Whenever decision situations arise, have your child identify the various choices before making the decision. Example: "Here are the choices you have for breakfast . . . " "What are the choices you can have for dinner at the restaurant?"

3. During a bedtime story, have your child identify the decision a character in their favorite book has to make. For example, what decisions could Goldilocks have made? Once inside the bears' house, what choices did she make concerning the porridge, the chairs, and the beds? Most fables, nursery rhymes, and young children books are extremely good sources for showing the difference between decisions and choices.

For young children ages 8 to 11:

1. Introduce the terms "decision" and "choice" to your child's vocabulary and the notions of "bigger and broader" decisions and "smaller and narrower" decisions. Give them a decision and have them tell you a related "bigger and broader" decision and a related "smaller and narrower" decision.

2. Whenever decision situations arise, hold the Focus Dialogue with your child. You can do this without proceeding through the entire FIVE-to-Decide conversation.

3. Ask your child what kinds of problems would "Skip the Quick" have with the Focus Dialogue? (See Chapter 5 for a description of Skip the Quick.) Follow by asking what your child's advice would be to help Skip the Quick do a better job with the Focus Dialogue.

For pre-teen and teenagers ages 12 to 15:

1. Ask your child, what is a decision? Let them struggle with the definition and then provide it to them using the term "choice" or "choices" in your discussion.

2. Introduce the notions of "bigger and broader" decisions and "smaller and narrower" decisions. Give them a decision and have them tell you a related "bigger and broader" decision and a related "smaller and narrower" decision.

3. Tell your teenager about a decision you have made and either

how you incorporated the concepts of the Focus Dialogue or how you could have incorporated the concepts.

4. Discuss with your child how peer pressure can affect or impact the Focus Dialogue.

5. Ask your child what kind of problems would "Skip the Quick" have with the Focus Dialogue? (See Chapter 5 for a description of Skip the Quick.) Follow by asking what your child's advice would be to help Skip the Quick do a better job with the Focus Dialogue.

For teenagers and young adults 16 and older:

1. Use the exercises 1 through 5 listed above for pre-teen and teenagers.

2. Introduce the notion of short-term consequences and long-term consequences associated with the choices of a decision and the need to consider both short-term and long-term consequences in decision making. Give examples such as the consequences associated with going on to a university or college.

3. Ask your child about a recent decision he or she made and have him or her reflect on how the concepts of the Focus Dialogue were incorporated or could have been incorporated.

The Focus Dialogue Guide

"Look up, look down, then all the way around."

Objective

You need to consider different perspectives on what is the decision to be made before agreeing on the specific decision to focus on. That is, you need to decide on what the right decision is. Once the decision is clearly defined, identify the distinctly and significantly different alternatives you feel should be considered (i.e., the choices to involve) in the subsequent dialogues that will lead to the decision. Creating a list of compelling choices is the ultimate goal of this dialogue. Getting the decision focus right will help ensure you address the right issues, solve the right problems, and consider all of the best possibilities.

Step-by-Step Dialogue Guide

Step 1: Declare "It's Time to Make a Decision" and Identify the Decision the Child Thinks Should be Made—

(a) Either the *parent or child* senses that it is time to start a decision-making conversation and explicitly makes this clear to the other. Example: *Parent: "I think it's time to make a decision on this issue. Let's start the Focus dialogue."* or *Child: "I need help in making up my mind about something. Can you help me Focus?"*

(b) *Parent: "What do you think is the decision you (or we) need to make?"* Parent and child discuss and then create a clear statement of the decision based on the initial issue or decision the child has introduced. Remember to keep in mind that a decision is a commitment of a valuable and limited resource or resources that can't be used for something else. Let's take an example: Should I go to David's birthday party that I have been invited to on Saturday afternoon?

Step 2: Agree on the Decision to Make—

(a) *Parent: "What do we do in the Focus dialogue?"*
Child: (with parental coaching as needed), "Look up, look down, then all the way around."
Parent: "Look up means, consider a related 'bigger and broader decision.' What do you think is the bigger decision?" Child and parent now discuss and create a clear definition of what the bigger and broader decision is. Example: How should I spend my Saturday afternoon (as opposed to going to the birthday party or not)?

(b) *Parent: "Look down means, consider what might be a related 'smaller and narrower decision.' What do you think is the smaller decision?"* Child and parent discuss and create a clear definition of what the smaller and narrower decision is. Example: How should I get to David's birthday party on Saturday afternoon?

(c) *Parent: "We have identified three different perspectives (decisions) as ways to think about the situation. Are there any other decisions or ways we should consider as the possible best approach to think about this situation?"* Child and parent should discuss the possibility and definition of any other potential decisions, like how should our family spend Saturday afternoon?

(d) *Parent: What do you think is the best way to think about the decision? Which of these decisions seem to provide the best perspective and why?* Child and parent need to discuss and agree to the best perspective and decision to focus on. Let's assume we have decided the proper decision focus is: How should I spend my Saturday afternoon?

Step 3: Identify the Choices for the Decision—

Parent: "Then all the way around means we need to consider the distinctly and significantly different choices that we can choose from for this decision. What do you think the choices are?" Child and parent now discuss and agree to a set of distinctly different choices for the decision in focus. For example, for "How should I spend my Saturday afternoon?" we can: (1) Attend David's birthday party, (2) Go with mom, dad, and sister to visit Uncle Dan, (3) Attend scheduled basketball practice, or (4) Attend scheduled basketball practice and then go late to David's birthday party.

Step 4: Quick Check: Do the choices feel right? Do we have the right focus?–

Parent: "Do the choices feel right? Do you think we have the right focus?" Starting with the child's perspective, the child and parent now have a discussion on whether the choices feel right. If something feels inappropriate in the previous discussion revisit the resulting choices and make adjustments as required.

Troubleshooting Guide–Frequently Encountered Sources of Difficulty

	Issue	Suggestion
1	I (parent) feel it is time to make a decision but my child is hesitant to start addressing the issues or decisions at hand.	Propose to start the series of discussions in the FIVE-to-Decide Conversation to determine where you run into difficulties. This will help you identify where to focus your efforts to become decision-ready for a subsequent conversation.
2	I (parent or child) am uncomfortable, embarrassed, or don't know how to start the conversation.	Start by saying that you are uncomfortable talking about this issue. The other will most likely be willing and open to help getting the conversation started. Use a metaphor to get started.
3	I (parent or child) can't think of a related "bigger and broader" decision.	The "bigger" decision is not always obvious nor needed; but, attempting to identify it is a critical step towards ensuring you focus on the right decision at this time. Try considering the perspectives of other individuals impacted by the decision and how they would think about the issue and situation.
4	I can't think of a "smaller and narrower" decision.	Similar to above. (same comment)
5	It seems like there are only two choices–either "we do it or we don't".	Don't forget timing and how much. Many yes/no decisions can be redefined to include options about timing or degree.
6	I (parent or child) am finding it difficult to choose, or agree on, the best decision perspective to take forward in the process.	Don't get hung up here. Ultimately, what you need to accomplish in this discussion is to create a list of compelling choices. If you are stuck in defining the decision, try going straight to listing choices. Once you are in agreement on the choices, there is no need to go back and define the decision.

Focus Dialogue Traps To Avoid

1. **Diving In**—Start discussing solutions or actions we should take before we take the time to consider what are the issues that we need to address. Ultimately, there needs to be a clear statement of the decision or decisions that need to be made; or at a minimum, agreement on a set of choices to consider.

2. **Premature Focus**—Starting with an initial definition and perspective of the decision and not stepping back to consider different decisions and perspectives that may provide a better way and better insights into thinking about the situation.

3. **Parental Browbeating**—The parent asking the questions and ultimately answering the questions throughout the course of the dialogue, not listening and appropriately responding to the verbal and non-verbal cues of the child.

4. **Hurrying**—Either the parent or the child pushing the dialogue faster than is appropriate, significantly reducing the quality of the discussion. This is especially problematic for the first few times you are having a decision-making conversation. Speed will come later as both the parent and child become more skilled in the process.

5. **Advocacy**—The parent or the child is approaching the discussion from that of an advocate for a particular decision definition, decision alternative (choice), or solution as opposed to approaching the discussion from that of a learning and discovery frame. This can lead to solving the wrong problem.

7

The Information Dialogue:
"What makes the decision hard or tough?
What information is *just* enough?"

Mother: So we agree that the decision we have is how to best spend your free time after school during the week. And the three choices you have are: (1) play on the afternoon school soccer team, but stay up later to do your homework on weekdays with no TV watching, and spend a little more time on homework on weekends; or, (2) not go out for the soccer team and devote more time to studying during the week so that you can have more free time on the weekend; or, (3) just continue with your same schedule of activities. Does that sound right?

Denise: Yes. That sounds about right.

Mother: Do you think the decision is easy or hard to make?

Denise: It's not that hard for me. I think I should join the soccer team.

Mother: Are you really sure playing soccer is something you're going to enjoy? You haven't played in a few years. It's going to be very competitive. I like the idea of you getting more exercise and playing a team sport. That's all good. I just hope you enjoy it.

Denise: Mom! I'm going to enjoy it, especially with Cindy being on the team.

Mother: *Are you sure Cindy is going to be on the team? Don't both of you have to go through tryouts to get on the team?*

Denise: *They don't have enough people on the team. There's no problem getting on the team.*

Good decision making requires information. In an age of information overload, the question becomes what information do you *really* need to make a decision—no more and no less. There are clear biases that show up here. Some individuals seem to require little or no information to make a decision, while others seemingly can't ever get enough, like "Debra Detail" introduced in Chapter 5. The key question is, *"What information is* just *enough?"*

> *Claire's Comment:*
> The Information Dialogue is where you put all your issues, concerns, and questions on the table. You really have to dig deep within yourself for this. The *must-learn* concept of this chapter is how to categorize each of these thoughts as either: assumptions, uncertainties, or issues of value.

Denise's mother seems to have concerns about whether or not Denise will enjoy playing on the soccer team, given she can make the team with Cindy. From the last chapter we know that Denise's mother also is concerned about the adverse impact on Denise's grades from spending time on soccer rather than school work. Information and insight on these concerns would really help make the decision easier to make.

For "Tom's Birthday Decision" in Chapter 6, the key information they would like to have is whether or not it will rain on Saturday. But they won't know for certain if it rains on Saturday until Saturday. How should they deal with that uncertain event?

In this chapter, we will be providing guidance on getting the right information for making the decision in focus—the Information Dialogue.

What Makes the Decision Hard or Tough?

Answering the question, "What makes the decision hard or tough?" uncovers the information needs of the decision *and* issues of value—the latter we touch on here but will address in more depth in Chapter 8. Is there something we can understand better or find out prior to making the decision that would make the decision easy or easier to make? For instance, will Denise and Cindy succeed in tryouts and make the soccer team? Or, will Denise truly enjoy being on the soccer team?

Next, are there value tradeoffs that need to be made? In this case, there are. Playing on the soccer team will be fun but could negatively impact Denise's grades. Denise and her mother will need to deal with the value trade-off between having fun and getting good grades.

In our example, Denise's mother seems to be the driver in raising the issues and concerns. This is not unusual as often times children are in an advocacy mode trying to "sell" a favorite choice. The Information Dialogue represents a great opportunity for parents to teach their children the critical thinking required in raising issues, concerns, and questions related to making a decision. Start by having your child answer the question "What makes the decision hard to make?" and then add your perspective after your child has addressed the question.

A good second question to ask is, "Is there anything else you would like to know to help you make the decision?" Often this question will raise important uncertainties that need to be addressed. In our example, the troubling uncertainty already raised by Denise's mother was the potential negative impact on Denise's grades resulting from playing soccer during time usually devoted to studying. If Denise and her mother knew the answer to this question it would reduce the difficulty of their decision regarding Denise's use of her free time.

How Much Information Is Enough?

Information—*for decision making*—has absolutely no value if it doesn't impact your choice for a decision. This seemingly obvious statement can manifest itself in subtle ways in business, often eluding business executives until it is spelled out. In our example, if Denise actually prefers studying to watching TV or being on the soccer team with Cindy, then the decision is easy. Knowing the potential negative impact on Denise's grades resulting from playing soccer is not relevant in their decision in this case since the obvious preferred choice becomes the second alternative—not to go out for the soccer team and devote more time to studying during the week so that you can have more free time on the weekend.

However, since it is clear that Denise prefers to play on the soccer

DON'T!

> Don't be like Debra Detail:
> • How might Debra Detail make the Information Dialogue difficult or confusing?
> • How would you help Debra keep on track and focus only on information that would truly help to make the decision?
> • Is there a little Debra Detail in you or your child?

team with Cindy rather than continue with her current schedule of activities or increasing her study time during the week, we understand that the potential negative impact on her grades from playing soccer *is* material to the decision. Is there any other information that will make either the decision easy to make or impacts the ultimate choice?

If the answer is yes, then Denise's mother should continue the dialogue with Denise, attempting to identify the information need. Otherwise, if the answer is no, Denise and her mother have identified the issues, concerns, and questions—collectively called the information needs—of the decision, which is the case in this situation. The information needs include: (1) will Denise and Cindy succeed in trying out for the soccer team? (2) how much will Denise enjoy being on the soccer team? and, (3) what will be the impact on Denise's grades resulting from playing on the soccer team?

Assume Only What Is Assumable

A constant problem in business settings is the assuming away of all the key uncertainties that may affect a decision. Assumptions are things that we take for granted, or an unstated belief. What we often call assumptions are, more often than not, desires or wishes about the future. The old maxim, "wishing doesn't make it so," is very appropriate when it comes to decision making. Once examined, critical assumptions are often more appropriately recast as uncertainties:

- "We decided to invest in real estate because properties in our neighborhood have been appreciating at double digit rates the last few years."
- "We enrolled our son in an accelerated program to help him get into a better university."
- "We changed soccer leagues because our daughter wasn't getting enough playing time in the games."

The statements above are troublesome because each includes an assumption about the future that is most likely an uncertainty. Will real estate prices continue to appreciate or cool down or possibly depreciate? Accelerated academic programs are great, but they are extremely competitive. Can the student do well in an accelerated program? What are the university admission rates for students in accelerated programs who perform modestly or poorly? Will changing the soccer league really result in more playing time for the daughter, or is there a different issue and decision that should be addressed?

Will Denise and Cindy succeed in trying out for the soccer team? Will Denise truly enjoy playing on the soccer team? Denise and her mother will have to decide whether these questions can be addressed as assumptions or should be addressed as uncertainties.

Identifying what you don't know and can't assume that is *material* to making the decision is a central part of the Information Dialogue. If it is uncertain at the time of the decision, then it should be treated as uncertain.

> *Claire's Comment:*
> I have a real simple assumption test. State your assumption, then see if you can think of a realistic situation that makes your assumption false. If you can, then your assumption is wrong. Keep your eyes open for bad assumptions. They seem to be everywhere once you start looking for them.

Assumption or Uncertainty?
List and categorize your information needs

Once you have completed discussing the two questions about what makes a decision hard and what if anything else do you need to know to make a decision, you should categorize each issue, concern, or question raised as either: (1) an assumption; (2) an uncertainty; or, (3) an issue of value that will be treated in the Value

Categorize, at most, one issue, concern, or question as an uncertainty.

It is important to reserve the category of uncertainties only for issues and concerns with potential outcomes that significantly change the perceived value of a choice. As an example, the uncertainty of whether or not it rains at the park during Tom's birthday party significantly influences Tom's enjoyment of the party. Consequently, the issue of the weather at the park the day of Tom's birthday should be classified as an uncertainty.

In many of your decisions, there will be no issues and concerns that need to be identified and treated as an uncertainty. To keep the FIVE-to-Decide process simple and manageable, identify at most *one* issue, concern, or question as an uncertainty. The implications of categorizing an issue, concern, or question as an uncertainty will become apparent in the Value and Evaluate Dialogues. Evaluating decisions with multiple uncertainties requires skills beyond the scope of this book.

Dialogue and the Evaluate Dialogue which we discuss in the next two chapters.

For every issue, concern, or question that you categorize as an assumption, express the assumption as simply as possible. If there is an issue, concern, or question that you categorize as an uncertainty, state the uncertainty as a question. And, for every issue, concern, or question you categorize as an issue of value, simply remember to address it in the Value and Evaluate Dialogues.

Claire's Comment:
If you are not sure whether one of your issues, concerns, or questions is value-related or not, chances are it is. So don't worry about it and simply mark it as value-related and think about it later in the Value and Evaluate Dialogues. Don't get stuck on it here.

Exhibit 7.1 provides a graphical overview of the Information Dialogue. The Information Dialogue lists and categorizes the information needs of the decision.

Mother: We have three information needs to deal with. First, will you and Cindy succeed in tryouts and make it on the soccer team? Second, how much will you enjoy being on the soccer team? And third, what will be the impact on your grades resulting from playing on the soccer team?

Exhibit 7.1: Graphical Overview of the Information Dialogue

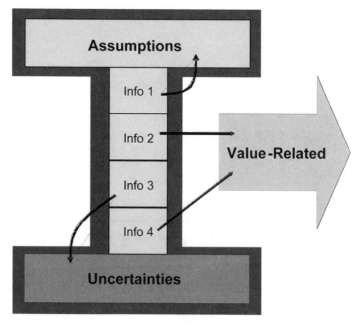

Denise: Those are *your* questions, not *my* questions.

Mother: Do you have different questions?

Denise: No. It's just that I know the answers to those questions, so they are not questions for me. We *will* make the soccer team. I *will* enjoy being on the team. And, I *will* keep my grades up.

Mother: Okay. Let's say that you are confident about each of those questions and maybe I am too. Let's just spend a little time on each of those and make sure. Okay?

Denise: Okay.

Mother: Let's start with the first question, will you and Cindy succeed in tryouts and make it on the soccer team?

Denise: The answer is yes. The coach is worried about having a team at all because not enough people are signing up.

Mother: So we can *assume* you and Cindy will make the team?

Denise: Absolutely!

Mother: Alright, let's make that an assumption. The next question is, will you really enjoy being on the soccer team? That is a question of value since it has to do with your preferences, so we will address this when we talk about value (in the Value Dialogue). The last question is, what will be the impact on your grades resulting from playing on the soccer team?

Denise: The time I will be at soccer practice is not time I usually spend on studying. So I don't think that playing soccer is going to impact my grades.

Mother. But playing soccer is going to be tiring, and by the time you get home you may not have as much energy to devote to studying.

Denise: *Mom*, I promise I will keep my grades up.

Mother: Denise, I know you will try your best to keep your grades up. I'm just not sure that will always be possible with such a full schedule. I think that there will be some impact on your grades, hopefully not much. I just don't think that is a good assumption. Since we prefer good grades to bad grades, this is a concern about preferences and value. We will address this when we talk about value. [Note: this concern could be addressed as an uncertainty; however, Denise's mother chooses not to do so.]

Denise: Is that it?

Mother: I think so. Have we uncovered and discussed all of our issues and concerns? Do you think we have categorized them right?

Denise: I think we have all the issues; but, I'm not sure about how we categorized them.

Mother: Don't worry. If we haven't got it right, it will become apparent when we talk about values and do the evaluation. We can always make changes then.

Would you agree with the conclusions of the above discussion? In the Information Dialogue you will be raising issues, concerns, and questions and determining how to address them in the context of making decisions. While you may or may not agree with the categorizing that Denise and her mother did, it is important that you realize the nature of the conversation. Each issue, concern, and question was addressed one at a time with a conclusion drawn on how best to proceed in incorporating it into the decision-making process. Exhibit 7.2 illustrates the results of the Information Dialogue for Denise and her mother.

In this example, Denise and her mother did not categorize any of their issues, concerns, or questions as uncertainties. Tom's Birthday Party Decision will illustrate an Information Dialogue with an uncertainty. To keep the overall FIVE-to-Decide Conversation manageable, you should categorize at most one issue, concern, or question as an uncertainty.

Exhibit 7.2: Results of Denise's Information Dialogue

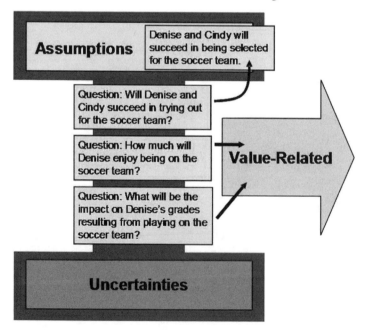

Tom's Birthday Party Decision—The Information Dialogue

Father: We have two choices for your Saturday birthday party: (1) have your birthday party in the park, but go to the arcade if it rains; or, (2) have your birthday party at the arcade and have some laser tag sessions. Is this decision easy or hard to make?

Tom: It's a little tough. I really want to have my party in the park, but if it rains then that messes everything up.

Father: What is making the decision hard?

Tom: Rain, Dad! It all depends on whether it rains or not.

Father: That's right. How you value a party in the park depends on whether or not it rains. Does anything else make the decision hard to make? How do your friends feel about the difference between a party at the park and a party at the arcade?

Tom: I don't think they care. They'll like either one.

Father: What else makes the decision difficult for you?

Tom: Nothing.

Father: Alright. Well, I have an issue. I believe the arcade requires a deposit for birthday parties, about 50 bucks. There is a 48-hour window on cancellations. If we cancel with less than 48 hours before your party, the arcade will keep the $50.

Tom: Really?

Father: Yup. So that's an issue. Is there anything else you would like to know to help you make the decision?

Tom: I don't think so.

Father: Okay. It sounds like there are four information needs we should deal with: First, how do your (Tom's) friends feel about a party at the arcade including laser tag versus a party at the park? Second, how do you (Tom) feel about a party at the park if it rains? Third, will it rain at the park on Saturday either before or during your party? And last, if we cancel a party at the arcade on Thursday or later we will lose the $50 deposit. [See Exhibit 7.3a.]

Father: Let's start with the first question, how your friends feel about an arcade party versus a park party.

Tom: My friends will like laser tag a lot. But I'm just tired of that place.

Father: So we can *assume* your friends will like an arcade party just as much as a park party?

Tom: I think so.

Father: We need to understand how you feel about a party in the rain. That's an issue of value and we'll come back to that a little later.

Tom: All right.

Father. Now, whether or not it rains at the park, is that an assumption or uncertainty?

Tom: That's for sure an uncertainty!
Father: Yeah. I agree. And the cancellation fee is an issue of value.
Tom: Is that all we need to know?
Father: Good question. Have we uncovered and discussed all of our is-
sues, concerns, and questions? And are we confident we have catego-
rized them right?
Tom: I think so. It feels right to me.
Father: Me too. [See Exhibit 7.3b.]

As you will see, the Information Dialogue will create a smooth
transition into the Value Dialogue. The Value Dialogue will take
each of the potential choices resulting from the Focus Dialogue and
use the information needs resulting from the Information Dialogue
to create the potential outcomes—end result—of the various decision paths. Each of these potential outcomes will be assessed for
value to support the child and parent in understanding and identifying the best decision choice based on value.

Exhibit 7.3a: Issues, Questions, and Concerns for Tom's Birthday Party Decision

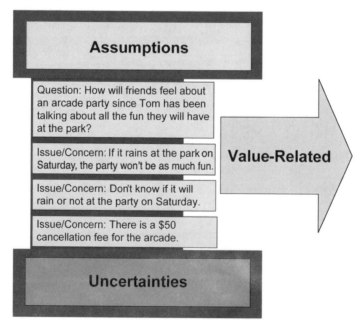

Exhibit 7.3b: Results of the Information Dialogue for Tom's Birthday Party Decision

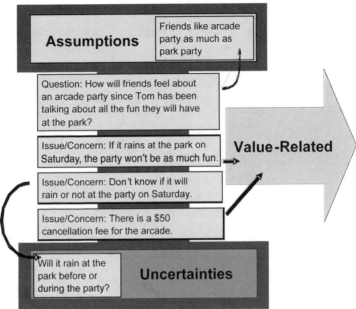

Getting Started

The Information Dialogue is all about being clear on what you would like to know to help you make the decision. Not everything you would like to know to help you make the decision can be known prior to making the decision. That is why we must introduce the notion of uncertainty. We will deal with the accounting of uncertainty later in the Value Dialogue and the Evaluate Dialogue. That is, how should we deal with information that is uncertain? At this point, we only are trying to identify the information needs.

Having a pen and paper pad to take brief notes will help you make sure that the issues raised are all addressed. You probably won't have a problem remembering your issues, but you may have a hard time keeping track and addressing well the issues your child raises. Remember, you are having a dialogue . . . not a monologue or lecture!

Think back to a decision you recently made. What assumptions did you make? Were any of the assumptions really uncertainties? Now consider a decision you are currently contemplating. What are the information needs? What assumptions can you make? What, if any, are relevant uncertainties? Over the next few days, pay attention to the conversations you are having with others and see if you can identify the assumptions being made. Ask yourself, "Are these really assumptions or uncertainties?"

Don't forget to take advantage of the characters introduced at the end of Chapter 5 (Claire Smart-Choice, Alan the Analyzer, Debra Detail, Frieda Fun Loving, Skip the Quick, and Timothy Timid) for explaining concerns you may have with your child's initial attempts at the Information Dialogue and subsequent dialogues discussed in the following chapters. Statements like, "Remember Debra Detail? Sometimes she makes this more difficult by thinking about *all* the questions she can think of rather than thinking about *only* the questions that will help us decide. Let's not be like that." Once again, by using the characters in your explanation we hope to create a more vivid image for your child, making your guidance easier to remember and more available.

Information Dialogue Summary

The Information Dialogue is an attempt to identify the issues, concerns, and questions relevant to making the decision. This can be achieved by addressing two questions:

1. What makes the decision hard or tough?
2. Is there anything you would like to know to help you make the decision?

In answering these two questions, both information-related issues and value-related issues will be identified. The information-related issues need to be each categorized as either an assumption or an uncertainty and made explicit by succinctly stating your assumptions and expressing your uncertainty as a question.

A high-quality Information Dialogue will accomplish four goals:

1. Raise all of the child's and parent's key issues, concerns, and questions regarding the decision;
2. Categorize each issue, concern, and question as an assumption, uncertainty, or an issue of value;
3. Result in no "bad" assumptions; and,
4. Include at most one uncertainty with consequences that impact which choice is most preferred.

If your Information Dialogue accomplishes these, you are ready to move on to the Value Dialogue.

Exercises

For very young children ages 4 to 7:

1. Play a game with your child of "True-False-Maybe." Make statements and ask your child if they are true, false, or maybe either. As an example, "Will we eat dinner tonight?" "Will it rain next week?" This will introduce the notion of uncertainty.

2. As you are driving your child home from school or an event, ask your child how many minutes it will take to get home. Once you get home, note how long it actually took to get home and discuss with your child the difference between her estimated time and the actual time. Estimation games will introduce the notion of uncertainty and help your child improve their ability to make estimates.

For children ages 8 to 15:

1. Explain and define for your child the concepts of assumption and uncertainty. Identify an event, perhaps something happening on the weekend and ask your child to provide you with example assumptions about the event and example uncertainties. As an example, consider a baseball game on Saturday. An assumption might be that it will start at 2:30 in the afternoon. An uncertainty might be, How long will the game last?

2. Continuing with the above discussion, you can ask your child what causes the identified uncertainty to be uncertain. As an example, the number of runs scored in the game impacts how long it will last.

3. Think about a recent decision you made. What assumptions did you make? Were any of those assumptions false? Were there uncertainties associated with the decision? If yes, what were they? Explain these thoughts to your child and ask your child to try and reflect on a past decision of their own and to analyze the decision as you have.

4. Ask your child what kinds of problems would "Skip the Quick" or "Debra Detail" have with the Information Dialogue? (See Chapter 5 for a description of Skip the Quick and Debra Detail.) Follow by asking what your child's advice would be to help Skip the Quick or Debra Detail do a better job with the Information Dialogue.

For teenagers and young adults 16 and older:

1. Use exercises 1 through 4 listed above for children ages 8 and older.

2. Have a discussion about attending a college or university after their graduation from high school and ask them about their issues, concerns, and questions regarding this. Categorize the issues, concerns, and questions as assumptions, or uncertainties, or value-related. You may find yourself having a great conversation about college attendance.

The Information Dialogue Guide

"What makes the decision hard or tough? What information is just *enough?"*

Objective

You need to identify and understand the issues, concerns, and questions that make the decision hard to make. Answering the question, "why is the decision easy or hard to make?" will uncover the information critical to making the decision and will illuminate the issues of value that need to be addressed (later, in the Value Dialogue). Ultimately, issues must be classified as either: (1) an assumption; (2) an uncertainty; or, (3) value-related.

Step-by-Step Dialogue Guide

Step 1: Why is the Decision Easy or Hard to Make? List Your Issues, Concerns, and Questions (collectively called "information needs")—

(a) *Parent: "What is the Information Dialogue all about?*
Child: (with parental coaching as needed), "What makes the decision hard or tough? What information is just enough?"
Parent: "Do you think this decision is easy or hard to make?"

(b) If the child proposes that the decision is easy, discuss and understand why the child believes this is the case. *Parent: "Why do think the decision is easy?"* If the parent and child mutually agree that the decision is easy, make the decision, and stop here. If the parent feels that there are issues, concerns, or questions that have not been dealt with (either in information that would be helpful to make the decision, or whether the child is thinking clearly about values—the child's and others', or whether the child has considered the breadth of consequences of the decision), then the parent should introduce those concerns now and discuss them with the child. Example: "Have you considered the consequences of missing basketball practice? What happens if you miss practice?"

(c) If the child proposes that the decision is hard or tough to make, discuss with the child why that is the case. *Parent: "Why do you think that the decision is hard?"* Try to be comprehensive here. Try to get the whole list of issues, concerns, and questions out 'on the table". This is a great opportunity for the child to communicate their perspective on the decision. Discuss each of the child's issue/concern/question only to the point that the parent understands what the issue/concern/question is. Don't debate them here. *Parent: "What else makes this decision difficult for you?"* Once the child has expressed their entire list of issues/concerns/questions and the parent understands each of these, then the parent should introduce any additional issues/concerns/ questions that they have. Start by going though the child's list and using statements like "I agree that we should consider how this decision impacts your sister's Saturday activities and what she wants to do." Parent should introduce each of their issues/concerns/questions without engaging in debate on any one. *Parent: "Is there anything else you would like to know to help you make the decision?"* Once the child has heard the parent's issues, this final question provides the child the opportunity to respond to the parent's list or add more of her own. This question will often elicit important uncertainties that need to be addressed.

Step 2: Categorize Information Needs as "Assumptions" or "Uncertainties" or "Value-Related"—

(a) *Parent: "Let's look at each issue (concern/question) and determine whether we should: 1) make an assumption about it; 2) treat it as an uncertainty; or, 3) call it an issue of value and deal with it in the Value Dialogue."* Child and parent review each issue one at a time and classify each issue as either an assumption, an uncertainty, or value-related. After some discussion, you may find that a group of issues are really one issue. As a guideline, attempt to reserve the classification of an issue as an uncertainty for at most one issue. Example: The party is planned to be outside in the back yard. If it rains, the party will not be nearly as fun. This issue should be classified as an uncertainty since you cannot control whether it rains or not on Saturday, which will impact the value of an outdoor party. On the other hand, you may be completely confident that it will not rain at the party on Saturday and so make the assumption that it will not rain on the party. Example: If your child misses basketball practice on Saturday, he/she will not get to be a starter in next week's game. This should be classified as a 'value-related' issue since the issue will be how to weigh this negative-valued outcome with other positive-valued outcomes.

(b) *Parent: "For each issue we have classified as an assumption or uncertainty, let's be clear on what we mean. For each assumption let's say what the assumption is and if there is an uncertainty let's state it as a question."* Example: Will it rain at David's birthday party on Saturday afternoon?

Step 3: Quick Check: Are All Issues/Concerns/Questions Addressed and Addressed Correctly?—

Parent: "Have we uncovered and discussed all of our issues (concerns and questions)? Have we dealt with them correctly? Starting with the child's perspective, the child and parent have a discussion on how well they have dealt with issues/concerns/questions associated with the decision. Did you deal with all of the issues? Is an issue missing? If you made assumptions, are they solid assumptions? If there is an uncertainty, have you stated it as a question? Revisit any aspect of the Information Dialogue that doesn't feel right.

Troubleshooting Guide—Frequently Encountered Sources of Difficulty

	Issue	Suggestion
1	There seems to be more than one issue that is an uncertainty.	Choose the one issue that stands out as having the most impact on the value scores in the Evaluate Dialogue. Treat the remaining issues as assumptions.
2	There are more than two possible outcomes for an uncertainty, yet the "dialogue" only allows for two.	Many uncertainties have more than two possible outcomes. To keep the "dialogue" manageable, define a "generalized favorable" outcome using a combination of the outcomes and do the same for a "generalized unfavorable" outcome. This will be sufficient for getting to a high-quality decision.
3	We have a very long list (more than 5) of issues and concerns. It feels like we have made the whole process overly complex.	Agree on what the 2 or 3 biggest issues are and focus only on those. At the end of the process, revisit the list of issues you did not formally address and determine whether any of them are important enough to re-introduce into the conversation.

Information Dialogue Traps To Avoid

1. **Assuming Away the Problem**—Decision making and problem solving go awry when we make bad assumptions. Often assumptions are more about things we wish were true so we assume that they are true. Always double check on what assumptions you are making to be sure that they are assumptions and not uncertainties about future events.

2. **Parental Browbeating**—The parent asking the questions and ultimately answering the questions throughout the course of the dialogue not listening and appropriately responding to the verbal and non-verbal cues of the child.

3. **Hurrying**—Either the parent or the child pushing the dialogue faster than is appropriate, significantly reducing the quality of the dialogue. This is especially problematic for the first few times you are having a decision-making conversation. Speed will come later as both the parent and child become more skilled in the process.

8

The Value Dialogue: "What's 'good'? What's 'bad'? Let's ask Mom or Dad."

> *Wife:* With the kids getting old enough now, I'd like to start looking into going back to work.
>
> *Husband:* I thought we were going to wait until they were both at least into elementary school?
>
> *Wife:* I don't think we need to wait that long. Plus, I think we could really use the extra money. We just keep creeping more and more into debt.
>
> *Husband:* Well I should be getting a good raise this year.
>
> *Wife:* It's not just the money. I'm getting a little bored too. I actually miss the work scene. I miss being with adults.

Maybe you have had a similar conversation like this at your home, or at least you probably know of a couple who have struggled with this issue or a variation of it. Making decisions requires making trade-offs of things that we value, such as money versus family quality time versus personal fulfillment and enjoyment. We all struggle with *value trade-offs* at various times in our lives. When consulting, we often need to remind our clients that "You can have anything, but you can't have everything." The best we can do is to make choices that maximize our chances of getting the things we want most. But to do that, we must understand what we want, and that's an issue of value.

The purpose of the Value Dialogue is to reveal the types of value (for example, personal enjoyment or money) that we should consider when we evaluate the choices associated with a decision. Learning to think broadly and comprehensively about value is yet another essential skill to becoming a good decision maker. This chapter is about identifying the types of value that we should incorporate into our personal decision-making process and that is applied in the Evaluate Dialogue—the topic of the next chapter.

Claire's Comment:
The Value Dialogue is pretty straightforward. There is only one *must-learn* concept and that is, what types of value should be considered in your decision and from whose perspective. Make sure you are comfortable with this concept and try it on a few decisions before you move into the optional sections of this chapter.

There's one last thing. Don't be too alarmed if this chapter serves as a bit of a wake-up call to the critical importance of *value*. After reading this chapter, you may find that your recent decision making may seem too narrowly focused with respect to certain values. We hope this chapter helps you get on track with your own personal decision making and makes you all the better as a mentor in teaching your children about value and value trade-offs.

What Are Values and Preferences?

According to the fourth edition of *The American Heritage Dictionary of the English Language*, the word *value* means "worth in usefulness or importance to the possessor; utility or merit: as in *the value of an education*." Critical to this definition is that value is perceived at a personal level. In other words, value is subjectively "in the eye of the beholder." According to the same source, *preference* means "the state of being preferred" where the root word, prefer, means to like better or value more highly. Preferences and value work *together* in making decisions.

Parents wield enormous influence on their children's perception of value and preferences since parents are the initial role models for their children on how to think about value, what has and does not have value, what is preferred over that which is rejected, and ultimately, what we assign as the value of the outcomes (consequences) of our choices. In this chapter, we are going to concentrate on identifying values, and leave the issue of preferences (i.e., which has a priority over another or the strength/ degree of a value) to the next chapter.

Many choices in our lives are bounded by personal ethics, religious beliefs, and norms in our society. In short, we need to be clear with our children from a very young age on issues and specifics regarding what is "right" and what is "wrong." Establishing these moral boundaries and the impact they have on our choices and valuing the consequences of our choices is a highly significant step towards becoming a good decision maker—maybe the most important one. Choices involving or resulting in stealing, dishonesty, deceit, or injury to others (including those that are unintentional because the full range of effects of certain choices is not fully appreciated) are not acceptable.

In the FIVE-to-Decide Conversation, we believe that issues of ethics, morality, and religion are best addressed as implicit and explicit boundaries in our choices established during the Focus Dialogue in Chapter 6 rather than associated with the value types in the Value Dialogue or value scoring performed in the Evaluate Dialogue in Chapter 9. In other words, some choices are out of bounds before we even start the conversation, and some, like those involving ethical dilemmas, should be resolved during the Focus Dialogue—the identification of choices—rather than during the Value Dialogue.

Categorizing Value

Assessing the value we personally place on an outcome or consequence requires us to think broadly and comprehensively about the ways we personally perceive and receive value. Below is a list of *categories of value* we suggest you should consider in the FIVE-to-Decide Conversation. The list is intended to be comprehensive with little or no overlap across categories. If there is a category of value you think is missing, add it to the list for consideration in all your future decisions that you apply the FIVE-to-Decide Conversation process.

The categories of value include:

- Enjoyment (fun)
- Health (well-being of you and others)
- Safety (and, on the contrary, hazard)
- Learning (formal and informal education)
- Family Quality Time (time nurturing the bonds of the family through events and activities among family members)
- Charity (helping others)
- Pain (physical or emotional)
- Money (wealth, cost, profit)
- Personal Fulfillment (apart or beyond enjoyment, learning, charity, and money)

- Time (the amount of time committed to an action)

Not all of these categories of value are appropriate for each decision. The Value Dialogue is intended to identify which categories apply to the specific decision at hand and from whose perspective—the child's, the parent's, or someone else's. Getting your children, and yourself, to consider all the sources of value associated with a decision is yet again another skill that needs to be learned and internalized into your decision making. For children, we can think of these categories of value as a set of boxes, each containing an inventory of a specific type of value.

"What's 'good'? What's 'bad'?
Let's ask Mom or Dad."

The phrase, "What's 'good'? What's 'bad'? Let's ask Mom or Dad" is our cue for the FIVE-to-Decide Conversation to shift into identifying the different categories of value to be considered for the decision at hand. Note that when we say "good," we are really talking about a situation or outcome that is positive, desirable, or favorable. Similarly, "bad" means something that is negative, undesirable, or unfavorable. Good and bad should not be interpreted as being moral or ethical terms in this context.

Therefore, the essence of the Value Dialogue is to:

1. Determine which categories of value (value types), for example, enjoyment, health, money, etc., should be applied during the Evaluate Dialogue—the next chapter's dialogue; and,

2. Identify from whose perspective you will be perceiving the value for each type of value under consideration (e.g., the child's perspective, the parent's perspective, the family's perspective).

We can increase the depth and sophistication of our Value Dialogue by the addition of two *optional* steps, which can be used with children who are 8 years old and older:

3. Establish how much "weight" the child will actually have in making the decision, i.e., how much *decision equity* will the child have for the decision?

4. Determine whether the degree of value, for any of the value types being applied in the decision, will depend on the outcomes (i.e., the resulting situation) of any uncertainty identified during the previous Information Dialogue. We call this

the *"It Depends" Clause*. For example, the enjoyment of a party in a park depends on whether it rains. If this is the case then,

a. Define what would be the "favorable outcome" and conversely, the "unfavorable outcome" associated with a decision choice (for example, a "favorable outcome" for a party at the park would be that it did not rain at the park both before and during the party on the day of the party).
b. Assess the "chances out of 100" that the "favorable outcome" will occur and conversely, the "chances out of 100" that the "unfavorable outcome" will occur.

Let's see how these steps work:

Mother: We need to identify which types of value are important to us for this decision and from whose perspective. Pick one of the choices and tell me which value types you think are important for that choice.

Denise: I'll start with playing on the soccer team and staying up later to do my homework.

Mother: Sounds good. What value types should we consider for that alternative?

(The Mother shows or describes to Denise a list of value categories.)

Denise: Well, fun for sure, we're going to have a great time on the soccer team.

Mother: Is that it?

Denise: No . . . Health is important too. We'll be getting a lot of exercise.

Mother: You're right. I'm sure you will. Is there any other type of value we should be considering?

Denise: Well . . . No, I don't think so.

Mother: I think there is a least one other type of value, and that is learning. There is a potential negative impact on your learning if you don't keep up with your studies. I also thought about safety from the perspective of you getting hurt. But, I think there isn't much of a chance of you getting seriously hurt.

Denise: I don't think it's going to impact my grades. And I agree that safety isn't an issue here.

Mother: Okay. Tell me, from whose perspective should we be considering those value types?

Denise: That's pretty easy. It would be *my* fun and *my* health, and I guess *my* grades (learning).

Mother: I think it is that easy. I agree. Let's check the other choices to see if we need to add some other types of value into consideration. How about the second choice; that is, not going out for the soccer team and devoting more time to studying during the week. What do you think? Do we need to add anymore value types for that choice?

Denise: Well if I'm not going out for soccer, it seems like the only thing we are talking about are my grades.

Mother: Certainly learning (grades) could be impacted. And I agree with you that we don't need to add any additional value types to cover that choice. How about the third choice, just continuing with your current activities? Do we need to add any additional types of value to cover that choice?

Denise: No, I think we are still covered.

Mother: I agree. *Your* enjoyment, *your* health, and *your* learning are the three types of value we should consider.

If Denise's mother wanted to include the concept of decision equity in this discussion, this would be a good point in time to do so. In this example, we will not apply and include decision equity; however, we do include it in "Tom's Birthday Party Decision" at the end of the chapter. Notice also that there was no uncertainty identified in the previous Information Dialogue so there will be no "It Depends" Clause required. However, in the example at the end of the chapter, you will see how that is used.

In this example, the child, Denise, identified two types of value, enjoyment (fun) and health (exercise); and her mother has added learning (as in grades and education). Each of these types of value will be considered from Denise's perspective, that is, *Denise's* fun, *Denise's* health, and *Denise's* grades and education.

For children, you can think of both the child and the parent each selecting the types of boxes of value to consider in anticipation of evaluating the choices. Exhibit 8.1 illustrates this value type selection process as the child first loading onto the conveyor belt the values he/she believes are important to the decision and the parent adding

> Don't be like Frieda Fun Loving:
> • How does Frieda's narrow focus on personal enjoyment limit her Value Dialogue?
> • How would you help Frieda think broadly about the types of value to use in a decision?
> • Is there a little Frieda in you or your child? That is, do some value types always come to mind while you (or your child) tend to overlook considering some other important types of value in your decision making?

Exhibit 8.1: The Value Types Denise and Her Mother Selected for Their Decision

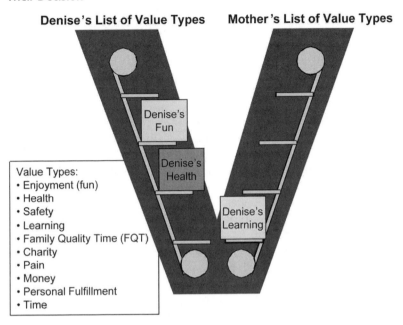

any value type they think is important the child has overlooked. Remembering to identify from whose perspective the value is being perceived is an important part of the discussion.

The following topics—decision equity, decision empowerment, and the "It Depends" Clause—are considered optional in that they are not necessary elements of a FIVE-to-Decide Conversation. However, as you and your child become more confident in the basic approach, you will find these topics to be valuable additions to your decision making. You may want to consider the following sections after you have a good handle on the overall FIVE-to-Decide Conversation. The following sections are for children as young as eight years old.

Decision Equity and Decision Empowerment (optional topic for children as young as 8)

By the time you and your child have delved into the Value Dialogue, the decision perspective has been established, the issues and concerns surrounding the decision have been identified, and the ways to think about and incorporate value are being discussed. It is at this point in time that the gravity of the situation and decision are becoming quite apparent and clear to both the child and the parent. The issue at hand is to what degree will you empower your child to make the decision at the conclusion of the FIVE-to-Decide Conversation. How much "say" or "weight" do you want your child to have in ultimately making the decision?

If your intent is to allow your child to make the decision at the end of the conversation, that is, to fully empower your child to make the commitment to a course of action, then you are giving them 100 percent of the *decision equity* for the decision. If, on the other hand, you intend to have a good conversation with your child about the decision but at the end of the conversation *you* will make the decision, then you (the parent) have 100 percent of the *decision equity* for the decision.

The FIVE-to-Decide Conversation process allows for the parent and child to explicitly account for decision equity in the evaluation of decision choices, the topic of the Evaluate Dialogue in the next chapter. During the Value Dialogue is a good point to establish how much decision equity (what percentage of 100 percent) the child will have in the specific decision under discussion. So, if you, the parent, would like to explicitly account for the split in decision equity between you and your child, then this should be discussed no later than the end of the Value Dialogue. The notion of decision equity is an important one. You may want to go back to Chapter 2 and refresh your understanding of this important topic.

The sum of the parent's decision equity and the child's decision equity must equal 100 percent.

A good strategy is to give your child an increasing *equity share* (something between 0 percent to 100 percent) in their decision making as your child matures and increases their skills in decision making so that by the time your child is fully empowered to make decisions—and is responsible for the resulting consequences—your child is an excellent decision maker. As you begin incorporating the FIVE-to-Decide Conversation into your and your child's decision making, you may initially start your child at somewhere around 10 percent to 25 percent decision equity (this implies you have 90 percent down to 75 percent respectively) for most of the decisions you are discussing; but always reserving the right to adjust their decision equity for any one decision. As your child improves in understanding and capability with decision making, you should increase their stake in the decision by increasing their equity share. Chapter 2 discusses the implications of your, the parent's, role in decision making as the balance of decision equity moves from you to your child.

As an example, if Denise and Denise's mother have been applying the concept of decision equity into their decision-making conversations, then Denise's mother might feel that their decision on Denise's use of free time should have a decision equity split of 50 percent decision equity for Denise and the remaining 50 percent decision equity for herself—the split Denise has worked up to at this point in time based on her level of skill in decision making and the maturity of her judgment. A 50/50 split in decision equity implies the parent is working as an equal partner with the child in making the decision.

The "It Depends" Clause (optional topic for children as young as 8)

Many of the difficult decisions we face in life are difficult because of some uncertainty involved. For example, if I take the job, will I like my new boss? If we purchase our home in that neighborhood, will it appreciate in value as much as our current neighborhood? If I buy this new car, will it be reliable? The "It Depends" Clause is a simple means to introduce and account for uncertainty in decisions. Children around the age of 8 typically understand this concept and can effectively use the "It Depends" Clause introduced here.

As you recall, during the previous chapter's Information Dialogue we identified and categorized issues as either: (1) an assumption; (2) an uncertainty; or (3) an issue of value. If an issue was identified as an uncertainty, we needed to determine whether any of the value types selected was impacted in their degree of value by the outcome of the uncertainty. In Tom's Birthday Party Decision, Tom's and his friends' enjoyment at the park is reduced if it rains. Consequently, with respect to enjoyment for the choice of a party in the park on Saturday, "it depends" on whether it rains at the park before or during the party on Saturday.

For our purposes, we will use the term "favorable outcome" and "unfavorable outcome" in discussing and applying the "It Depends" Clause. The idea is to think about the uncertainty and identify two situations or outcomes for the uncertainty—a "good" or favorable outcome and a "bad" or unfavorable outcome. Now, not all uncertainties are so easily split into two cases of favorable or unfavorable. In Tom's Birthday Party decision it is pretty black and white, either it will rain or it won't. What should you do if the uncertainty is cost, which has many—not just two—potential outcomes? In cases where the uncertainty has many possible outcomes varying in degree of favorableness, think about an important threshold value that splits the uncertainty into two cases. As an example, an uncertainty about cost can be split into a favorable outcome of less than or equal to $100 and an unfavorable outcome of more than $100. The importance of the $100 could be that anything less than or equal to $100 is what the family has budgeted or could afford and any amount more than $100 is deemed more than the family is willing or would like to spend.

Once a definition for a favorable outcome, and conversely, an unfavorable outcome has been established, you will need to assess the chance of the favorable outcome occurring and the chance of the unfavorable outcome occurring. To do this we think in terms of chances out of 100. The idea is to split 100 chances between the favorable outcome and the unfavorable outcome consistent with your knowledge and beliefs about the uncertainty.

Claire's Comment:
All of these statements about the uncertainty of rain mean the same thing. There is a 30 percent chance it will rain. There is a 70 percent chance it will not rain. There are 30 chances out of 100 that it will rain. The probability it will rain is 0.30. The likelihood it will rain is 30 percent.

The sum of the "chances of a favorable outcome" and the "chances of an unfavorable outcome" must equal 100 percent.

Let's demonstrate all of this by returning to the conclusion of the Information Dialogue on Tom's Saturday birthday party in Chapter 7.

Tom's Birthday Party Decision—The Value Dialogue

Father: All right. Let's have the Value Dialogue. What do we do here?

Tom: Yeah, yeah . . . What's good? What's bad? Let's ask Mom or Dad.

Father: Good. We're considering two choices: a birthday party at the park on Saturday or a party at the arcade including laser tag sessions. For information, we said we can assume your friends will like an arcade party just as much as a park party; we identified whether it rains at the park on Saturday as an uncertainty; and finally, we have an issue of value to account for and that's the $50 deposit for the arcade. Do I have everything?

Tom: I think so.

Father: Pick one of those choices and tell me what value types you think are important for that choice.

Tom: Let's start with the party at the park.
Father (showing Tom the list of value categories or listing them for Tom if Tom isn't familiar with the list): Okay. What types of value should we consider for that alternative?
Tom: That's easy. Enjoyment.
Father: Whose enjoyment?
Tom: My enjoyment . . . and my friends' enjoyment.
Father: All we need to concentrate on is *your* enjoyment.
Tom: But I won't enjoy the party if my friends don't.
Father: Exactly. That is why *your* enjoyment is a good value measure for this. *Your* enjoyment accounts for how your friends feel about it too.
Tom: Okay. I get it.
Father: Anything else? Any other type of value we should consider for the party at the park?
Tom: Nope.
Father: Your enjoyment at the party is important to me and your Mom. But also, the cost of this party is important too. Do you agree?
Tom: I guess it's important for you. But you'll have to decide if you want to pay for it.
Father: You're right. So we're going to use *your* enjoyment and *my* cost in thinking about value. Does that make sense?
Tom: Yes.
Father: How about having an arcade party?
Tom: It's still all about fun. None of the other measures are important here . . . at least for me.
Father: And how much it is going to cost *me*. I think we are set on the types of value to include for this decision.

Father: We've been splitting decision equity on this as 40/60 with 40 percent for you and 60 percent for me and Mom. That still seems about right for this decision. What do you think about that?
Tom: That seems fair. Unless you want to go to 50/50?
Father: Nice try. You're getting there! But you and I are not quite yet at an even split.
[See Exhibit 8.2a.]
Father: Since we have an uncertainty to consider, let's see if we need to apply the 'It Depends' Clause. Does whether it rains on Saturday at the park impact how much fun you will have for either of the choices?
Tom: Of course! If I have my party at the park and it rains, it will be terrible.
Father: So how would you describe a 'good or favorable outcome'?

Tom: A good outcome would be it doesn't rain.

Father: So a 'good or favorable outcome' would be no rain at the park Saturday and an 'unfavorable outcome' would be rain at the park on Saturday. Do you agree?

Tom: Absolutely.

Father: What do you think the chances are that it will rain on Saturday?

Tom: I don't know. What do you think?

Father: Well, the weatherman was saying there is about a 30 percent chance of rain on Saturday. How about using his forecast, 30 percent, or 30 chances out of 100?

Tom: Sure. That works for me.

Father: That means we will be using 30 chances out of 100 for the unfavorable outcome of rain at the park on Saturday, and 70 chances out of 100 for the favorable outcome of no rain at the park on Saturday. Did I get that right?

Tom: That's right.

Father: Okay. Have we identified all of the sources (types) of value for the choices we are considering? Both positive and negative?

Tom: I think we're okay. It's *my* fun and *your* money. It's pretty simple.

Father: All right. Let's Evaluate our choices. [See Exhibit 8.2b.]

Claire's Comment:

If you and your child disagree over the "chances out of 100 of a favorable outcome", don't argue about it now. Wait until you complete the Evaluate Dialogue! During the Evaluate Dialogue, try using both your uncertainty assessment (chances out of 100 of a favorable outcome) and your child's uncertainty assessment. If your evaluation of the decision choices using your uncertainty assessment indicates the "best" choice is the same as "best" choice from your child's evaluation using their uncertainty assessment, then the difference in your opinions on the uncertainty assessment doesn't matter. However, if the indicated "best" choice is different depending on whose uncertainty assessment is used, then you should re-think and discuss your "chances out of 100 of a favorable outcome."

Exhibit 8.2a: The Value Types Tom and His Father Selected for Their Decision and Their Decision Equity Split

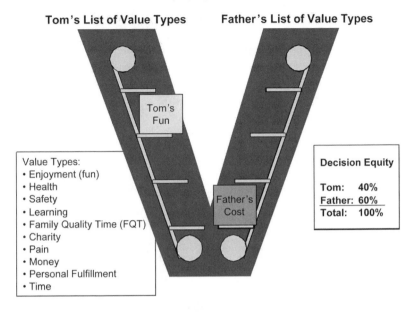

Exhibit 8.2b: Tom's and His Father's Use of the "It Depends" Clause for the Uncertainty of Rain at the Park on Saturday

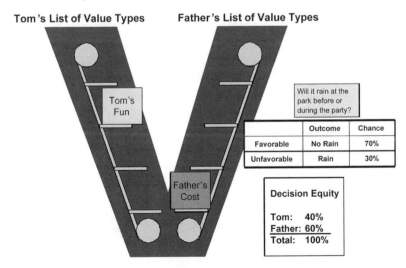

Getting Started

Thinking broadly and comprehensively about value is going to take a little effort. You and your child will need, at least initially, some physical reminder of the value types (perhaps a card with the list of value types) that should be considered for inclusion in the Value Dialogue and then later in the Evaluate Dialogue. If your children are old enough to include the "It Depends" Clause in your *FIVE-to-Decide Conversation* but you find it a bit clumsy at the beginning; don't apply the clause in your discussions until you and your child are comfortable or have mastered the portion of the Value Dialogue related to identifying the value types.

For yourself, reflect on recent decisions you have made and determine whether you excluded an important value type during the decision process. Alternatively, is there a specific value type that has been driving your decision making? Review our list of value types and determine if you would like to revise the list in any way to better reflect your personal views and beliefs. Also, try out the "It Depends" Clause for yourself either by reflecting on a past decision you made or a current decision you are facing.

For your child, have a discussion regarding the different types of value and integrate it with important messages you have for your child on morals, beliefs, and expectations. Agree on the list of value types that you want to use in your and their decision making. If your child is ready for dealing with uncertainty in decision making, practice applying the "It Depends" Clause on hypothetical situations or discussing a recent decision that resulted in a "bad outcome." For example, your child's decision to participate in an extra-curricular activity has resulted in not enough time for homework, which in turn resulted in lower than expected grades. And finally, discuss with your child the notions of decision empowerment and decision equity. Explain to them that your goal is to help them become good decision makers and that as they improve in judgment and decision-making skills, you will allow them to have more and more decision equity.

Once again, don't forget to take advantage of the characters introduced at the end of Chapter 5 (Claire Smart-Choice, Alan the Analyzer, Debra Detail, Frieda Fun Loving, Skip the Quick, and Timothy Timid) for explaining concerns you may have with your child's initial attempts at the Value Dialogue and other dialogues discussed in these chapters. Statements like, "Remember Frieda Fun Loving? Sometimes she doesn't think about all the ways she gets value from a choice. She always thinks about how fun something is but sometimes forgets about family quality time or how much things cost. Let's not be like that." By using the characters in your explanation we hope to create a more vivid image for your child, making your guidance easier to follow and remember.

As with every dialogue within the FIVE-to-Decide process, practice is required to make it a natural part of your conversations and decision-making process.

Value Dialogue Summary

The Value Dialogue is intended to:

1. Determine what categories of value (example: enjoyment, health, money) should be applied during the Evaluate Dialogue—the next dialogue; and,

2. Identify whose values and preferences should be accounted for when considering each value type (example: child's fun and parent's cost).

For children as young as 8 years old:

3. (Optional) Establish how much "weight" the child will actually have in making the decision (how much decision equity will the child have for the decision?)

4. (Optional) Determine whether the degree of value, for any of the value types being applied in the decision, will depend on the outcomes (i.e., the resulting situation) of any uncertainty identified during the previous Information Dialogue. If this is the case then,

    a. Define what would be the "favorable outcome" and conversely, the "unfavorable outcome" associated with a decision choice.

    b. Assess the "chances out of 100" that the "favorable outcome" will occur and conversely, the "chances out of 100" that the "unfavorable outcome" will occur.

A high-quality Value Dialogue accomplishes three goals:

1. Identifies all of the sources of value (both positive/"good" and negative/"bad") associated with the decision's choices and potential consequences of those choices from both the child's perspective and the parent's perspective;

2. Assesses the chances of a favorable outcome for any uncertainty identified during the Information Dialogue that could result in situations that impact the degree of value for one or more of the value types selected;

3. Feels intuitively right for both child and parent.

If your Value Dialogue accomplishes these, you are ready to move on to the Evaluate Dialogue.

Exercises

For very young children ages 4 to 7:

1. Introduce the word "value" to your child's vocabulary by defining it with words they will understand and providing them with examples.

2. Introduce the value types that your child is capable of understanding and then state situations or events and have your child categorize the type of value associated with the situation or event. (For example, eating an ice cream cone—fun. Getting a shot at the doctor's office—health. Playing a game on the playground with friends—fun and health.)

3. Create your personalized value types list to use for you and your child by eliminating or adding value types to the list offered in this chapter.

For young children ages 8 to 11:

1. Introduce the word "value" to your child's vocabulary using the definition in the chapter and providing them with examples.

2. Introduce and discuss the list of value types provided in the chapter and then state situations or events and have your child categorize the type of value associated with the situation or event. (For example, eating an ice cream cone—fun. Getting a shot at the doctor's office—health. Playing on a soccer team—fun and health.)

3. Create your personalized value types list to use for you and your child by eliminating or adding value types to the list offered in this chapter.

4. Introduce the concept of numerically assessing uncertainty by asking questions like, "what are the chances out of 100 that we will get home before 6:30 tonight" as you drive home from soccer practice? Or, "what are the chances out of 100 that (you fill in their favorite professional sports team) will win first place in their division this year?"

5. Whenever decision situations arise, hold the Value Dialogue with your child. You can embed this into a complete *FIVE-to-*

Decide Conversation or engage in just the Value Dialogue to assist you and your child in thinking broadly about value when considering choices.

6. Ask your child what kinds of problems would "Frieda Fun Loving" have with the Value Dialogue? (See Chapter 5 for a description of Frieda Fun Loving.) Follow by asking what your child's advice would be to help Frieda Fun Loving do a better job with the Value Dialogue.

For pre-teen and teenagers ages 12 to 15:

1. Ask your child, what is value? Let them struggle with the definition and then provide it to them using the definitions for value and preferences in the chapter.

2. Introduce and discuss the list of value types provided in the chapter and then state situations or events and have your child categorize the type of value associated with the situation or event. (Ex: Eating at their favorite fast food restaurant—fun. A visit to the doctor's office—health. Playing in the school orchestra—fun and learning. Playing on an after-school basketball team—fun and health.)

3. Discuss whether the value types list provided in the chapter is complete. Ask your child if they think anything is missing from the list. Discuss and agree on your personalized value types list to use for you and your child.

4. Introduce the notion of the "It Depends" Clause and provide examples. Ask your child to contemplate a recent decision they made and describe how they could have used the "It Depends" Clause.

5. Introduce the concept of numerically assessing uncertainty by asking questions like, "what are the chances out of 100 that we will get home before 6:30 tonight" as you drive home from orchestra practice or basketball practice? Or, "what are the chances out of 100 that (you fill in their favorite professional sports team) will win first place in their division this year?"

6. Have a conversation about decision empowerment and decision equity including your personal thoughts and beliefs on this topic with respect to raising children.

7. Whenever decision situations arise, hold the Value Dialogue with your child. You can embed this into a complete *FIVE-to-Decide Conversation* or engage in just the Value Dialogue to assist you and your child in thinking broadly about value when considering choices.

8. Ask your child what kinds of problems would "Frieda Fun Loving" have with the Value Dialogue? (See Chapter 5 for a description of Frieda Fun Loving.) Follow by asking what your child's advice would be to help Frieda Fun Loving do a better job with the Value Dialogue.

For teenagers and young adults 16 and older:

1. Use the exercises 1 through 8 listed above for pre-teen and teenagers.

2. Discuss how issues of morality and ethics are included best as boundaries in choices—the Focus Dialogue rather than as values and preferences in the Value Dialogue.

3. Have a discussion about whether and how the values and preferences of others should be included in an individual's decision making.

4. Ask your child about a recent decision he or she made and have him or her reflect on how the concepts of the Value Dialogue were incorporated or could have been incorporated.

The Value Dialogue Guide

"What's 'good'? What's 'bad'? Let's ask Mom or Dad."

Objective

You need to identify whose values and preferences should be accounted for in making the decision and what types of value are important to those individuals and therefore should be considered in making the decision. When the value of an alternative depends on an information-need that was identified as "uncertain" during the Information Dialogue, then you will need to apply the "It Depends" Clause during the next step, Evaluate. In preparation for the application of the "It Depends" Clause, you will need to define what is meant as a "favorable" outcome and an "unfavorable" outcome for the uncertainty and assess the chances of getting a "favorable" outcome and the chances of getting an "unfavorable" outcome.

Step-by-Step Dialogue Guide

Step 1: Identify Which Values Should Be Applied and from Whose Perspective (for One Choice)—

(a) *Parent: "What do we do in the Value Dialogue?"*
Child: (with parental coaching as needed), "What's 'good'? What's 'bad'? Let's ask Mom or Dad."

Parent: "Pick one of the choices and tell me which value types you think are important for that choice." Child pick's one of the choices from the Focus Dialogue and identifies which value types (enjoyment [fun], health, safety, learning, family quality time, charity, pain, money, personal fulfillment, and time) are important for that choice. Example: For a sleepover at a friend's house the value types might be fun and safety. After the child has offered their opinion on the list of value types to consider, the parent should offer their thoughts and suggested additions or modifications.

(b) *Parent: "From whose perspective should we be considering for each of the value types for this choice?"* Child offer's their opinion on whose perspective should be applied for each of the value types for the choice under consideration. Example: For a sleep-over decision, fun would be from the child's perspective and safety would also be from the child's perspective. After the child has offered their opinion on whose perspective, then the parent should offer their thoughts and suggested additions or modifications. Both the parent and child should be comfortable with the conclusions of this discussion before moving on to another choice.

Step 2: Repeat Step 1 for the Remaining Choices and (Optional) Agree on Decision Equity Split—

After identifying the list of value types for each of the choices identified in the Focus Dialogue, step back and review the list of value types in its entirety and check to determine if it is complete.

(a) *Parent: "Does our list of value types cover the set of choices we are considering?"*

(b) *Optional—Parent: "Now let's agree on how to split the decision equity or share."* Example: "Since everyone in the family will be impacted by this decision, I suggest you (child) should have half of the share and we (parents) take the other half"—that is, 50 percent share for the child and 50 percent share for the rest of the family. Or, "I want to leave this decision mostly up to you (child). So how about you (child) take 80 percent of the share and I'll take 20 percent. What do you think?" Discuss this until you reach an agreement.

Step 3: Do We Need the "It Depends" Clause? If Yes, Assess the Chance of the "Favorable" and "Unfavorable" Outcomes—

(a) *Parent: "Let's check to see if we need to use the "It Depends" Clause.* Briefly scan the choices to determine whether a value score for any one of the choices will depend (or change) on the outcome of an information need you have classified as uncertain. If this is the case, then you will need to apply the "It Depends" Clause. Example: How much fun the child will have at an outdoor party on Saturday will depend on whether or not it will rain.

If you don't need to apply the "It Depends" Clause, go to Step 4.

(b) Using the "It Depends" Clause means you need to imagine two (and only two) different future situations that summarize the potential outcomes of the "uncertainty"
identified in the Information Dialogue. Define the favorable (preferred) outcome as
an event where the uncertainty is resolved in a favorable way and the unfavorable
(less preferred) outcome as an event where the uncertainty is resolved in an unfavorable way. *Parent: "Okay, let's describe a favorable outcome and then an unfavorable
outcome based on the uncertainty."* Child and parent first discuss and agree on the
definition of the favorable outcome based on the potential outcomes of the uncertainty and then define the unfavorable outcome. Example: Favorable Outcome—It
does not rain at David's birthday party on Saturday afternoon. Unfavorable Outcome—It does rain at David's birthday party on Saturday afternoon.

(c) *Parent: "What do you think the chances are that the favorable outcome, (state the favorable outcome), will occur?* How many chances out of 100? Given there are 100 total
chances, how many chances out of 100 would the child assign to getting the favorable outcome? Example: "What do you think the chances are that it does not rain at
David's birthday party on Saturday?" Child: "I think there are 70 chances out of 100
(70 percent chance) that it will not rain." Parent: "So that means you believe there
are only 30 chances out of 100 (30 percent chance) that it will rain at the party on
Saturday. That's consistent with the weather forecast for the weekend. I agree." If
the child has difficulty providing an assessment, the parent should provide their assessment and discuss it with the child. If the child and the parent disagree on the assessment, record both and test both during the Evaluate Dialogue.

**Step 4: Quick Check: Have You Identified and Accounted for All of the Sources of Value (Pos-
itive and Negative)? If You Used the "It Depends" Clause, Are You Confident You Used
It Correctly?—**

*Parent: "Have we identified and accounted for all of the sources of value both positive [good]
and negative [bad] for you? Have we done the same for myself and anyone else whose values
and preferences we are considering in this decision? Are you confident that we used the "It Depends" Clause appropriately (given it was used)?* Starting with the child's perspective, the
child and parent now have a discussion on the questions above. If something feels inappropriate in the previous discussion, identify the concern, discuss, and make adjustments as required.

Troubleshooting Guide—Frequently Encountered Sources of Difficulty

	Issue	Suggestion
1	We are having difficulties identifying a "favorable" outcome and an "unfavorable" outcome because the uncertainty has many possible outcomes. Example: How long it will take to drive across town during rush hour?	For uncertainties that have numerous possible outcomes define two representative outcomes—one as a "favorable" outcome and another as "unfavorable." In the example of time, consider the "favorable" outcome as "getting somewhere on time" or "getting there in an hour or less". In these cases, the respective "unfavorable" outcomes would be "arriving late" and "getting there in over an hour".
2	The parent and the child disagree on the chances out of 100 for the favorable outcome.	Record both assessments and use both assessments in the Evaluate Dialogue to determine if it makes a difference in determining the "best" choice.
3	We have a value type (ex: fun) that applies to both my child and myself. How should we handle this?	Consider having two separate value measures for fun—one for the child and one for the parent.
4	We (parent of child) think we have a value type that is not available in the list. How can we add it?	The list of value types is intended to be comprehensive, yet you may have still another value type you would like to add. Feel free to tailor the list of value types to fit your personal situation and preferences. However, many issues you may consider as a value type may be better treated as assumptions or built into the alternatives under consideration (examples: love, regret, ethics).

Value Dialogue Traps To Avoid

1. **Double Counting**—The value types are intended to create mutually exclusive categories of value that should be assessed independent of one another. Be careful not to double count a sense of value in more than one category.

2. **Neglecting a Key Stakeholder**—Be sure to think carefully and prudently about whose values and preferences should be associated with a value type. Others who may be included for their personal preferences for a given value type include: relatives, close friends, organization members, and teammates.

3. **Parental Browbeating**—The parent asking the questions and ultimately answering the questions throughout the course of the conversation, not listening and appropriately responding to the verbal and non-verbal cues of the child.

4. **Hurrying**—Either the parent or the child pushing the conversation faster than is appropriate, significantly reducing the quality of the conversation. This is especially problematic for the first few times you are having a decision-making conversation. Speed will come later as both the parent and child become more skilled in the process.

5. **Advocacy**—The parent or the child is approaching the discussion from that of an advocate for a particular choice, biasing the discussion in ways that create a rationale for their desired choice.

The Evaluate Dialogue:
"Let's do the math to find the best path."

> **Mother:** *Okay. We're going to decide on how you should best use your free time. We agreed that there are three types of value that we need to consider in making the decision: (1) your fun (enjoyment), (2) your health, and (3) your education (learning). Do I have it right?*
>
> **Denise:** *Yes.*
>
> **Mother:** *We need to determine which one of the choices is the best with respect to these three types of value. We need to understand the value story underlying the best choice.*

The Evaluate Dialogue is the point at which we pull all together the results of the previous FIVE-to-Decide Dialogues and make an evaluation of each decision choice. You can take several different approaches in this dialogue, and it is important that you choose an approach that is appropriate

Claire's Comment:

The Evaluate Dialogue is about figuring out which of the choices is best based on the child's and parent's perspective of value. There are two *must-learn* concepts and they are: (1) determining which evaluate approach is best for your child and you, the parent; and, (2) how to uncover the reasons why one choice is better than the others—the value story.

Don't feel you have to use an approach that requires numbers and math to have a good Evaluate Dialogue. In fact, even if you are comfortable with the math, you may want to start with the simplest no number, no math approach until you are good at creating value stories.

for your child and for you, the parent. The approaches range from using no numbers or math at all to fairly sophisticated mathematical approaches. The best approach for you and your child is the approach that you and your child are most comfortable in applying. Using more sophisticated mathematical approaches does not necessarily imply a better Evaluate Dialogue.

In this chapter, we will discuss four approaches to having the Evaluate Dialogue. We will start with the simplest approach—no numbers or math—and then add tools and degrees of mathematical sophistication to the subsequent approaches.

Understanding the Best Value Story

Ultimately, the Evaluate Dialogue answers the question, "Is one choice clearly the best choice?" The Evaluate Dialogue should reveal the underlying *best value story*. That is, what is a best choice and why is a particular choice the best choice? The Evaluate Dialogue draws from and synthesizes all of the previous dialogues. In doing so, it is often the case that you will rethink and perhaps redefine your choices at this stage of the FIVE-to-Decide Conversation. In some cases, at this point of the FIVE-to-Decide you will feel that the best choice is obvious—which, remember, is the ultimate goal of the exercise.

In this dialogue, you have several different choices on how to proceed to create the value story. Approach 1 does not require the use of value-scoring systems and math. Approaches 2, 3 and 4 will require value-scoring systems and math with increasing degrees of mathematical sophistication.

Sounds like a mouthful, doesn't it? But it isn't really. We will be providing you a systematic way on how to think about and score decision choices based on the value types important for the specific decision. And if you would rather not use a scoring system, we will provide guidance on how to have a good Evaluate Dialogue that will reveal the best choice for the set of decision choices you and your child have created in the Focus Dialogue. However, we believe that if you and your child are comfortable in applying a scoring system, in many cases you will significantly improve the quality of your Evaluate Dialogue.

"Let's do the math to find the best path"

The essence of the Evaluate Dialogue is contained in three actions:

1. Assess the value for each decision choice accounting for the value types identified in the Value Dialogue.

2. Ensure that all of the issues, concerns, and questions identified in the earlier Information Dialogue have been addressed either in the choices, or as an assumption or uncertainty, or in the value types.

3. Given mutual (child and parent) satisfaction with the breadth and detail of the previous dialogues, the objective of the Evaluate Dialogue is to evaluate each of the choices and understand why the best choice is preferred to all other decision choices. This is what we call the "value story." Ultimately, all of our decision dialogues—the Focus, Information, Value, and Evaluate Dialogues—must enable us to answer the question, "Is there *one choice* that is clearly the best choice of all those available to us?"

If you used either the "It Depends" Clause or the concept of decision equity in your Value Dialogue for your decision, then you will need to apply the appropriate next step(s) as introduced below. These additional steps can be used for children as young as 8 years old.

4. If decision equity was introduced in the Value Dialogue, then the child's and parent's decision equity percentages need to be included in determining the value score for each decision choice.

5. If the "It Depends" Clause was used in the Value Dialogue, then a value score will need to be assessed for both the "favorable outcome" and the "unfavorable outcome" associated with a decision choice (for example, the enjoyment of a party in a park depends on whether it rains).

The phrase, "Let's do the math to find the best path" is the cue for the FIVE-to-Decide Conversation to shift into evaluating the choices and associated outcomes of those choices identified in our previous dialogues.

Evaluate Approach 1: Evaluating Choices
Without Numbers or Math

For a variety of reasons, you may not want to use a numerical approach for the Evaluate Dialogue:

1. Your child has not reached a level of maturity for a number-based approach to work.

2. You are having this dialogue in a vehicle while you are driving and writing numbers down on a scorecard really isn't a very smart thing to be doing at the moment.

3. You find using a number-based approach is clumsy and you are personally uncomfortable with it.
4. You just don't like driving your decision conversations with numbers.

Claire's Comment:
This chapter is filled with numbers and scoring systems. The fact is, you can have a very good Evaluate Dialogue and not use numbers at all. But to do that you need to follow the guidelines in this section. Some of my friends found it initially easier to learn the FIVE-to-Decide Conversation without using numbers and then later started using the value-scoring approaches after they were comfortable with each of the five dialogues in the FIVE-to-Decide Conversation.

If any of these reasons rings true, then this section is for you.

To have an Evaluate Dialogue without numbers or math, you and your child should do the following:

1. Review with your child the list of value types to be considered for each of the choices and from whose perspective for each value type.
2. Have your child consider all of the choices created during the Focus Dialogue and identify the "best" choice from the perspective of the value types under consideration. Then, have your child explain why the choice identified as "best" is the best by using statements that touch on each of the value types and contrasts the "best" choice with the other decision choices. This is the essence of the value story.
3. After your child has explained their perspective on the "best" choice, you, the parent, identify what you consider the "best" choice and provide an explanation just as your child has done—your perspective on the value story.

If you and your child are in agreement on the "best" choice, then you have probably had a sufficient Evaluate Dialogue. On the other hand, if you and your child disagree on what is the "best" choice, then you will have to have a deeper discussion on why you differ in opinion on the "best" choice. In either case, the goal is to get to the value story, even if you disagree on the "best" choice and value story.

Mother: Denise, which choice do you think is the best choice? What is the value story? Make sure you consider the three types of value: (1) *your* fun (enjoyment), (2) *your* health, and (3) *your* education (learning).

Denise: Well, I think going out for the soccer team is the best choice. Of the three choices it is the only choice that gets me exercising and I know you want me to start exercising. I can keep my grades up by giving up my TV watching during the week so there is no problem with school. Also, playing on the soccer team will be a lot of fun for me. I really think going out for the soccer team is the best choice.

Mother: You did a good job. You thought about each value type. I really think the key issue is whether or not you can keep your grades up. If you can keep your grades up either by giving up TV watching during the week or giving up whatever else distracts you from your homework, then I agree that going out for the soccer team is the best choice. It really is as simple as that.

A Simple Scoring System for Valuing Outcomes

The notion of assigning numbers or quantities to our values and preferences is a topic that academic researchers and business practitioners have developed extensively over the past two hundred years in the field of decision making. Our goal is to keep the assignment of numbers as simple as possible. More sophisticated approaches and techniques are possible within the FIVE-to-Decide Conversation, but these are not necessary for beginners. We will be using a three-point scoring system that is described in Exhibit 9.1.

Let's try an example. A child is evaluating the act of eating an ice cream sundae from the perspective of the value type *fun* (enjoyment). The key is to focus on the "interpretation" in Exhibit 9.1 rather than on the numerical score or the "description." With

Exhibit 9.1: Simple Three-Point Scoring System

Description	Score	Interpretation
High-Positive	3	Very, very desirable (good); extremely desirable (good); few things better than this
Medium-Positive	2	Very desirable (good); but not extremely desirable (good)
Low-Positive	1	Desirable (good); but no big deal
Neutral-Indifference	0	Neither desirable (good) nor undesirable (bad)
Low-Negative	−1	Undesirable (bad); but not a big deal
Medium-Negative	−2	Very undesirable (bad); but not extremely undesirable (bad)
High-Negative	−3	Very, very undesirable (bad); extremely undesirable (bad); few things worse than this

respect to "having fun," the child may say that having an ice cream sundae is a favorable (i.e., good or desirable) thing, but not a "very favorable" thing or an "extremely favorable" thing *when compared to all other activities that the child could do for fun.* Consequently, on the fun (enjoyment) scale, the child would value eating an ice cream sundae as having "one point." On the contrary, the same child might view a trip to Disneyland as an extremely favorable or desirable thing—few, if any, activities would be more fun than that. Consequently, on the fun (enjoyment) scale, the child would value a trip to Disneyland as a "three point" event.

For the value type *safety,* the child would probably score both eating an ice cream sundae or a trip to Disneyland as neither a favorable thing nor an unfavorable thing. Consequently, the child would score these two activities as both "zero" for the value type *safety.*

To improve on associating the most appropriate score for a decision outcome, both you and your child should attempt to visualize the outcome. Think about the joy of eating the ice cream sundae before value scoring it. Think about the day you would be spending at Disneyland and what you might be doing there before value scoring it.

Having a birthday party in a park sounds like a favorable or desirable thing. However, choosing to have a party in the park coupled with the unfavorable outcome of rain on that day at the park could result in a minus or negative "fun" value score for that decision and its outcome. Again, for discussions with your child and in thinking for yourself, focus on the "interpretation" words in Exhibit 9.1 rather than the numbers and visualize the outcome you are value scoring.

Claire's Comment:
The three-point system is easy to use. If you're measuring a good thing, something with positive value, then give it a score of "1" if it's good but no big deal. Give it a "3" if it is one of the best things you can think of for that value type. And give it a "2" for everything else in between. Use the same kind of thinking for negative scores of undesirable events.

How would you score an evening out with your significant other for the fun (enjoyment) value type with your children safely at home with a relative or good friend? If you score it a three, then you are not going out enough!

The simple three-point scoring system is applicable to all value types: enjoyment, health, safety, learning, family quality time, charity, pain, money, personal fulfillment, and time. *Your score is always made with respect to that particular value type.* For instance, a "3" for an activity for the health value type indicates that there are few, if any, other activities or events that have as healthy an outcome for the individual participating in the activity. Swimming, as a regular exercise, might score a "3" on the health value scale.

Evaluate Approach 2: Using a Decision Scorecard

Since most of our decisions have more than one value type (fun, family quality time, cost, etc.) associated with our choices, it is convenient to use a simple scorecard to record the value scores rather than to try to remember them as you go. Let's return to our example with Denise and her mother deciding on how Denise should use her free time. A simple scorecard for Denise's first choice is illustrated in Exhibit 9.2. For Denise's decision there are three scorecards, one for each of the choices including: (1) play on the after-school soccer team, but stay up later to do your homework on weekdays with no TV watching, and spend a little more time on homework on weekends; or, (2) not go out for the soccer team and devote more time to studying during the week so that you can have more free time on the weekend; or, (3) just continue with your current schedule of activities.

The "Comments" section of the scorecard is used for jotting down notes to help you remember the motivation behind a recorded value score. It is not mandatory, it is just there to help you keep track of why you decided to give a value a particular score. Notice—and this is very important—*that the "value type" section of the decision scorecard is always with respect to an individual or group as discussed in Chapter 8 (e.g., "Denise's Fun").*

For younger children, you may want to value-score the choices together and not separate the child's scoring from the parent's scoring. Consequently,

Exhibit 9.2: The Decision Scorecard for Denise's Decision

Choice 1	Value Type	Comments	Child's Value Score	Parent's Value Score
Play on After-School Soccer Team, but Stay Up Later to Do Homework on Weedays with No TV Watching and Spend More Time on Homework on Weekends	Denise's Fun			
	Denise's Health			
	Denise's Education			
		Total	0	0

the Decision Scorecard in Exhibit 9.2 would have only one column on the far right for value scores. The parent would lead the discussion and help teach the child about value scoring as the parent and child agree on the value score for each value type in the dialogue. Once the child is proficient in the concept of value scoring, then the Decision Scorecard with the child's perspective and the parent's perspective can be introduced as illustrated in Exhibit 9.2.

Additionally, for younger children, starting with the language in Exhibit 9.1 rather than the numbers is the best approach for teaching children about measuring value. As an example, asking your child, "Can you think of anything else that would be a lot more fun than (choice 1)?" will give you a sense of whether your child thinks the choice rates a 1, 2, or 3 for the enjoyment value type. Consequently, the parent can value-score all of the choices with the child and not use numbers or math at all in the discussion with the child.

Now let's return to Denise's decision and provide an example of using the Decision Scorecard.

Mother: Let's start with the choice of you playing on the after school soccer team and let's first consider how much fun you will have. Would playing on the soccer team be one of the most fun things you can think of doing?

Denise: No.

Mother: Well then would you consider it very fun or fun, but no big deal?

Denise: It's a big deal. I think it will be very fun. Especially with Cindy being on the team!

Mother: Sounds like you'd score that a 2. Do you agree?

Denise: Yes. I agree.

Mother: I think you will have a lot of fun. I'll score it a 2 as well.

Mother: Next, let's think about your health. How would you score playing on the soccer team for health?

> *Claire's Comment:*
> Don't get all caught up in just assigning the numbers. The most important part of this dialogue is understanding each other's thoughts behind the scores. The numbers don't mean anything if you can't explain your thinking behind the numbers.

Denise: Well, I'll be getting a lot of exercise. And you are always telling me that I need more exercise. So, I would score health as a 3, because I can't think of many other physical activities that I would consider that would have as much exercise.

Mother: That sounds reasonable. And I would agree with you from my perspective. So we both score that a 3.

Mother: There is one more value type to consider, learning (education). More specifically, how you will do academically during the soccer season. How would you score *your education* for the soccer team choice?

Denise: Mom! I promise I'm going to do my homework, just as I said I would. Plus, it's important to learn how to play on a team and be a good team member. I know it will be more difficult to keep my grades up, but I will. I score education as a one. This will have an overall positive impact on my education.

Mother: This is the part that I have some concern. Your grades have been down a little lately and I'm really worried about you not having enough time and attention focused on your academics. I know you have the best intentions. I'm just worried you are going to run out of steam at the end of the day. I think your grades could really suffer. I'm scoring your education as a negative 2. That's how I see it.

Now let's consider the second choice, not go out for the soccer team and devote more time to studying during the week so that you can have more free time on the weekend. How fun will that be for you?

Denise: Not as much fun, although, I will have more free time on the weekend to do stuff. I would score it a 1, no big deal but good.

Mother: Okay, so you score that a 1. And I understand that. From your perspective, I would score it a 1 as well. How about health? How would you score that?

Denise: I don't think it's a big deal either way. I don't think health is an issue. I would score it a zero.

Mother: Yes, but you are still not getting enough exercise. You really should do some form of exercise in your free time. For this choice, I'm scoring health as a negative 1. Do you understand why I'm scoring it negative?

Denise: No. Why?

Mother: Because you do need to get some exercise so any choice about how you spend your free time that doesn't have exercise as part of it I think is a bad choice—for *health*. Does that make sense?

Denise: Yes, it does. But that wasn't one of the issues you raised earlier in the Information Dialogue.

Mother: You're right. It wasn't. But as we are having the conversation I'm realizing that this is an important point. So it should have been one of my concerns in the Information Dialogue. So I am addressing it now with you and I'm including it in the evaluation. You know, this is just how the FIVE-to-Decide is intended to work. We can always go back and change things as we go since we are learning more about this decision each step of the way. Okay?

Denise: Okay. I understand.

Mother: Now, what about *your education*?

Denise: Well, I will be spending more time on my homework during the week. I don't think it is a big deal. I'm giving it a 1.

Mother: I think you will benefit from the additional focus on your studies. I'm giving it a 2. That extra effort will pay off for you.

Denise and her mother continued to discuss the third choice, having Denise continue with her same schedule of activities and their scores for this third choice along with the first two choices are provided in Exhibit 9.3.

As you see, total value scores for each alternative are determined by merely adding the value scores. In this case, Denise places the most value on the first choice, playing on the after school soccer team, with a total score of 6 points. Although based on separate scores, Denise's mother also prefers the first choice, playing on the after-school soccer team with a total score of 3 points.

There are a few *guidelines* (not rules) you should apply that were part of the above discussion:

1. Child goes first in value scoring: The mother always had the child think through and provide her (Denise's) value score before the mother provided her thoughts and score. Remember, this is both a learning opportunity for the child and a great way for the parent and child to have a complete and open dialogue.

2. Parent provides parent's value score immediately after each of the child's value scores: To minimize confusion and to ensure a complete dialogue is being held for each value score provided by the child, it is best for the parent to provide their value score immediately after the child has provided their value score.

3. Don't argue over value scores: Remember, value scores are a personal preference. The parent needs to make sure that the child is applying the 3-point scoring system appropriately, but

Exhibit 9.3: Denise's Completed Decision Scorecard

Choice 1	Value Type	Comments	Child's Value Score	Parent's Value
Play on After-School Soccer Team, but Stay Up Later to Do Homework on Weedays with No TV Watching and Spend More Time on Homework on Weekends	Denise's Fun	It will be very fun to be on the soccer team.	2	2
	Denise's Health	The daily exercise will be great for Denise.	3	3
	Denise's Education	Learning to be a good team player is important. Mom is really concerned about not having enough focus on academics.	1	-2
		Total	6	3

Choice 2	Value Type	Comments	Child's Value Score	Parent's Value
Do Not Go Out for After-School Soccer Team, Devote More Time to Studying During the Week, and Have More Free Time on the Weekend	Denise's Fun	The extra free time on the weekend will allow for some fun activities.	1	1
	Denise's Health	Mom has concern about Denise not having enough physical activities.	0	-1
	Denise's Education	This is the best choice for positively impacting Denise's grades.	1	2
		Total	2	2

Choice 3	Value Type	Comments	Child's Value Score	Parent's Value
	Denise's Fun	Denise currently has free time and spends it on fun activities.	1	1
	Denise's Health	Mom has concern about Denise not having enough physical activities.	0	-1
Continue with Current Schedule of Activities	Denise's Education	Denise currently has enough time for her school work.	1	1
		Total	2	1

the parent should not be haggling with the child about the child's score.

In the previous example, the value scores were completed by decision choice. That is, all of the value scores for the "soccer team" choice were assessed and then the value scores for the "spend more week-day time on homework" choice were assessed, and finally the value scores for "continuing with the

> *Don't be like Alan the Analyzer:*
> • How might Alan the Analyzer overcomplicate this dialogue?
> • How would you help Alan keep on track and not overcomplicate this?
> • Is there a little Alan the Analyzer in you or your child?

DON'T! same schedule of activities." You may find that in some cases you may want to complete the value scoring by value type. That is, assess the value scores for "fun (enjoyment)" for all choices and then proceed with the value scoring of "health." Either sequence will work fine.

> Don't be like Skip the Quick:
> • What short cuts might Skip the Quick try to take here?
> • How would you help Skip keep on track?
> • Is there a little Skip the Quick in you or your child?

The example we provided here as an introduction accounted for three choices. For decisions with more than three choices, we merely have to add additional areas in the decision scorecard to allow for the additional choices. The scoring approach is unchanged with the exception of having additional value scores to cover the additional choices.

It is important to realize that the decision scorecard doesn't tell you what decision to make. It merely is an attempt to reveal and summarize the underlying value story of each of the choices.

There are still two more objectives of the Evaluate Dialogue, and that includes making sure all of the issues, concerns, and questions raised in the Information Dialogue have been dealt with and that the child and the parent understand the underlying "value story" for the preferred choice.

Let's return to Denise's decision scorecard to understand the value story of her decision. As depicted in Exhibit 9.3, Denise clearly values the "soccer team" choice over the other two choices by 6 points to 2 points. The story here is that Denise perceives so much more benefit from exercise and more fun under that choice than the other two choices. Denise doesn't expect much if any of a negative impact on her grades from spending much of her free time devoted to the soccer team.

Denise's mother believes that playing on the soccer team could negatively impact Denise's grades. On the other hand, Denise's mother also believes there is a great health benefit for getting Denise in an after-school sport like soccer that requires strong cardiovascular conditioning. Moreover, Denise's mother also realizes that Denise will enjoy this more than other free time activities she has been doing. Although Denise and her mother disagree in degree in their value scores, they ultimately agree on what is the "best" choice.

Now, let's continue with Denise's and Denise's mother's Evaluate Dialogue.

Mother: That's interesting. We both scored the 'soccer team' choice as the best choice. But before we discuss the 'value story,' let's make sure we have considered all the issues, concerns, and questions we raised in the Information Dialogue. We said, we would assume that you and Cindy will make the soccer team since the team needs more players. We addressed the issue of how much fun you will have on the soccer team as one of our value types during the evaluation. And I accounted for my concerns about your grades by using 'education' as a value type. I think we covered everything. What do you think?

Denise: I think so. And we actually agreed on the best choice in the evaluation!

Mother: And that leads us to the final step of the Evaluate Dialogue, and that is, what is the value story behind the 'soccer team' choice?

Denise: The value story is that playing on the after school soccer team is the only choice that provides me with a good exercise program. You are more worried about my grades being affected than I am. But even with that, you felt that my health and my fun outweighed the negative impact of soccer playing on my grades.

Mother: That's pretty good. That's a pretty thorough review of the value story. I'm a little surprised at the evaluation. But as I think about it, I'm feeling more comfortable. But there's a really firm commitment you're making Denise on the use of your time after soccer practice. And that's the next dialogue, the Decide Dialogue.

Exhibit 9.4 provides a graphical representation of the value scoring Denise and her mother performed on their preferred choice, having Denise play on the after-school soccer team.

The following topics—decision equity, decision empowerment, and the "It Depends" Clause—are considered optional in that they are not necessary elements of a FIVE-to-Decide Conversation. However, as you and your child become more confident in the basic approach, you will find these topics to be valuable additions to your decision making. You may want to consider the following sections after you have a good handle on the overall FIVE-to-Decide Conversation. The following sections are for children as young as eight years old.

Evaluate Approach 3: Using Decision Equity
(optional topic for children as young as 8)

When a child is fully responsible for making his or her own decisions, then we say that the child has 100 percent *decision equity—or is empowered to make decisions.* A person has full decision equity

Exhibit 9.4: Denise's and Her Mother's Value-Scoring of the "Play on the Soccer Team" Choice

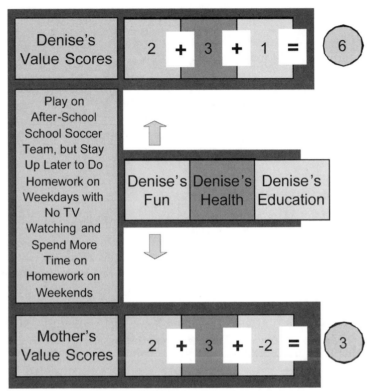

when the person has complete ownership of making the decision and full ownership of the resulting outcomes (consequences) of the decision. Just as ownership of a house or business, we can split decision equity between a parent and child. This notion has a nice mathematical application in our Evaluate Dialogue. If a child has 25 percent decision equity and a parent the remaining 75 percent of the decision equity, then we can apply these percentages in the evaluation to create one, fully comprehensive value score for any given choice by multiplying the child's value score by 25 percent (or 0.25) and multiplying the parent's value score by 75 percent (or 0.75) and adding these two values to get the one, fully-comprehensive score—a decision equity-based score.

The sum of the parent's decision equity and the child's decision equity must equal 100 percent.

As an example, if Denise has 40 percent decision equity and her mother the remaining 60 percent decision equity, then by applying the total value scores in Exhibit 9.3 we can calculate the decision equity-based value score for Denise's first choice, "playing on the after school soccer team" as:

After School Soccer Team Value Score =
(0.40 × 6) + (0.60 × 3) = 4.2.

We will leave it to the reader to verify that the decision equity-based value scores for Denise's second choice and third choice in Exhibit 9.3 are 2.0 and 1.4 respectfully. Based on this calculation, the best choice indicated by the evaluation would be for Denise to play on the after school soccer team since 4.2 is greater than 2.0 and 1.4.

For the Mathematically Savvy

(Optional topic for children and parents with quantitative interests; for others, skip to *Getting Started*.)

As noted in the previous chapter on the Value Dialogue, many decisions we face in life are difficult because of uncertainty. The "It Depends" Clause was introduced to allow the FIVE-to-Decide Conversation to account for uncertainty. As an example, enjoyment at the park is negatively impacted if it rains and positively impacted if it doesn't rain. Consequently, the degree of enjoyment we have at the park *depends* on whether it rains or not on that day.

Evaluate Approach 4: Using the "It Depends" Clause (optional topic for children as young as 8)

To apply the concept of a decision scorecard when uncertainty must be accounted, we need now to be explicit about the situations that create differences in our value scoring. Let's return to Tom's decision on the location of his Saturday birthday party and continue where we left off in the last chapter to demonstrate the use of a decision scorecard when applying the "It Depends" Clause.

Tom's Birthday Party Decision—The Evaluate Dialogue

Father: I'm going to set up our decision scorecard. Since we're applying the 'It Depends' Clause, we need to first be clear on what we are calling a 'favorable' or desirable outcome and conversely, what we are calling an 'unfavorable' or undesirable outcome.

Exhibit 9.5: Tom's Completed Decision Scorecard

Favorable Outcome:	It does not rain in the park on or before the party on Saturday.	Chance of Favorable Outcome:	70%

Unfavorable Outcome:	It rains in the park on or before the party on Saturday.	Chance of Unfavorable Outcome:	30%

Choice 1	Value Type	Comments	Outcome	Child's Value	Parent's Value Score
Birthday Party in the Park on Saturday	Tom's Fun	If it rains, Tom thinks it will be no fun moving the party to the arcade.	Favorable	2	2
			Unfavorable	-1	0
	Dad's Cost	Dad will pay arcade deposit just in case it rains to keep the arcade party option available. But the arcade party will be quite a bit more expensive.	Favorable	-1	-1
			Unfavorable	-2	-2
		10 is calculated by adding the "favorable" outcome scores (2 plus -1 which is equal to 1) and multiplying that by the chance of the "favorable" outcome~ as measured in points or chances out of 100~ (70) resulting in 70; and then adding the "unfavorable" outcome scores (0 plus -2 which equals to -2) and multiplying that by the chance of the "unfavorable" outcome (30) resulting in -60. The value of the alternative (the Value Weighted by Chance) from the parent's perspective is the sum of these two calculated numbers, 70 + (-60) which equals 10.	Favorable		
			Unfavorable		
			Favorable		
			Unfavorable		
			Favorable		
			Unfavorable		
			Favorable		
			Unfavorable		
		Total	Favorable	1	1
			Unfavorable	-3	-2
		Value Weighted by Chance		-20	10

Choice 2	Value Type	Comments	Outcome	Child's Value	Parent's Value Score
Birthday Party at Arcade with Laser Tag	Tom's Fun	The arcade party will not be as fun as the park party.	Favorable	1	1
			Unfavorable	1	1
	Dad's Cost	The arcade party is quite a bit more expensive than the park party.	Favorable	-2	-2
			Unfavorable	-2	-2
			Favorable		
			Unfavorable		
			Favorable		
			Unfavorable		
			Favorable		
			Unfavorable		
		Total	Favorable	-1	-1
			Unfavorable	-1	-1
		Value Weighted by Chance		-100	-100

Father: We said that a 'favorable' outcome would be 'it does not rain in the park on or before the party on Saturday,' so I'll write that down to help us remember it during our value scoring. [See Exhibit 9.5.]

Father: And for the 'unfavorable' outcome, we have that 'it rains in the park during the party or in the morning of the party on Saturday.' That is the uncertainty we wanted to address in this decision. Is that right?

Tom: Yes, that's it.

Father: Now in order to complete the evaluation, we will need to know the chances or likelihood of the 'favorable' outcome versus the chances of the 'unfavorable' outcome. What are the chances of the 'favorable' outcome, that is, the situation that is doesn't rain?

Tom: Well, we decided to use the weatherman's forecast of a 30 percent chance of 'rain' on Saturday.

Father: So are you comfortable using the weatherman's estimate?

Tom: I am. Are you?

Father: I am too. So the chance of 'rain' is 30 percent, which means there is a 70 percent chance it does not rain at the park on Saturday. [See Exhibit 9.5.]

The sum of the "Chance of a Favorable Outcome" and the "Chance of an Unfavorable Outcome" must equal 100 percent.

Father: From the Value Dialogue we agreed that there are two value types we need to consider: your enjoyment (fun) and the cost of the parties, which I'll be paying. Am I right?

Tom: You're right. I'm ready to score the choices.

Father: Okay. Let's start with the choice of having your birthday party in the park. And let's consider the case of the 'favorable' outcome; that is, it doesn't rain. What is your value score for your fun under that outcome?

Tom: It'll be very fun. I'd call it a 2 on the enjoyment scale.

Father: I agree. I think you and your friends will have a lot of fun. You've really been looking forward to this. I score it a 2 as well.

Father: What about the situation that it rains? Tom, how would you score 'fun' having a party in the park and it rains?

Tom: That is a disaster. That would be extremely unfavorable! So I guess that's a minus 3?

Father: Well let's think about that for a moment. If it rains at the park were not going to stay there. If we have paid the deposit for the arcade, we can just go to the arcade and move the party there. It won't be that big of a deal.

Tom: Okay. I wasn't thinking about it that way. That's not so bad. I mean it's unfavorable, but not a big deal. I'd score that a minus 1.

Father: Actually, I think even if we have to move the party to the arcade you'll have fun. But I realize it wouldn't be fun having to move in the middle of everything. So, I'm scoring this outcome as a zero, neither favorable nor unfavorable.

Father: Now, let's consider the other value type—the cost of the party at the park. You know, it is clear to me that what we should really do is to make the $50 deposit at the arcade regardless of our decision today. So even if it rains at the park we can move the party to the arcade. The cost of the party at the park won't be too much, even considering the $50 deposit.

Tom: It sounds like 'unfavorable, but not a big deal' applies.

Father: I think so.

Tom: It sounds like you would score the party at the park a minus 1.

Father: It's not quite that easy. Since it's about cost for me, it must be negative; but the cost of the party at the park choice *depends* on whether it rains. Does that make sense? What do you think the costliest situation is?

Tom: Probably having the party at the park but it rains and we move the party to the arcade.

Father: I think you're right. Some of the things that we would buy for the park party would not be usable in the arcade, and we'd end up spending money at the arcade too. Depending on how many laser tag sessions you and your friends do, the arcade activities will cost quite a bit more than the party at the park. So I'm scoring minus 1 on cost for a party at the park given it doesn't rain. And I'm scoring the situation of choosing the park party but then moving the party to the arcade because of rain a minus 2. Does that make sense?

Tom: It makes sense.

Father: So how would you score my cost of the party at the park?

Tom: It's your cost. I'd score it the same as you.

Father: Okay. We have value-scored the party at the park. And along the way we covered some of the value-scoring of the arcade party choice. Let's think about value-scoring your fun for the arcade party choice.

Tom: I've already said that I'd rather have the party in the park.

Father: I understand. So think about the language in the 3-point scoring system (Exhibit 9.1). Which statement best applies to an arcade party from your perspective regarding fun and enjoyment?

Tom: I'd like it, but it's no big deal. So that's a 1.

Father: That sounds reasonable. Since it doesn't really matter whether it rains or not with an indoor arcade party. We'll value-score the 'favorable' and 'unfavorable' outcomes the same for the arcade party choice. And I'm value-scoring your enjoyment at an arcade party the same as you did, a positive 1.

Father: Now we've actually already discussed the cost of an arcade party as we value-scored the park party choice. Remember the arcade party is going to cost quite a bit more.

Tom: So I'm value scoring that a minus 2.

Father: Yes, that would make sense and I'm doing the same.

Father: Great! Now all that is left for the evaluation is to do a little math to determine the *value weighted by chance* score for the two choices.

Father: Let's double-check to make sure we have considered all of the issues, concerns, and questions we discussed earlier in the Information Dialogue. Let's see, we assumed that your friends would like a party at the arcade as much as a party at the park. And, we dealt with the uncertainty of whether or not it rains at the park. And, we accounted for the $50 cancellation fee. I think we covered everything pretty well. What do you think?

Tom: I think so too.

Father: So there is one more thing to cover in the Evaluate Dialogue and that is the value story. Let's look at the evaluation and see if one of the choices is clearly the best choice and try to understand why? Is there a 'best' choice?

Tom: Yeah, I think so. Look, we both score having my party in the park higher than the arcade party. You score it as 10 points and I score it as –20. I guess I don't like either choice since my scores are –20 for the park party and –100 for the arcade party.

Father: That is funny. But remember, all we are trying to identify is the choice with the highest score. But you are right, our evaluations are consistent; we both scored the choice of having the party at the park with the option to go to the arcade if it rains as the highest value alternative. But why? What is the value story?

Tom: The value of the party at the park is having the option to move the party to the arcade if it starts raining. If we didn't have that option, the park party would score differently. We didn't evaluate that, but I bet if we didn't have the 'go to arcade if it rains' option, the park party would not have scored as well as the arcade party.

Father: I think that *is* the value story. Great job!

Value Weighted by Chance Calculation

To get a "total" value score for *FIVE-to-Decide Conversations* that use the "It Depends" Clause, we need to do a simple calculation once all of the value scores have been collected. We refer to this calculated value as the *value weighted by chance*. There are four steps to calculating the *value weighted by chance* that must be completed for each decision choice. These steps are completed separately for the child's scores and the parent's scores.

> **Step 1:** Add the value scores for the "favorable" outcomes.
>
> **Step 2:** Add the value scores for the "unfavorable" outcomes.
>
> **Step 3:** Multiply the result of Step 1 by the number of chances out of 100 chances of a "favorable" outcome occurring. (We use a 100-point scale to indicate chance or uncertainty. In other words, we think of the number of chances out of a total of 100 chances. If we say there are 70 chances out of 100 chances that an event will occur, this is equivalent to saying there is a 70 percent chance that the event will occur.)
>
> **Step 4:** Multiply the result of Step 2 by the chance of an "unfa-

Exhibit 9.6: Graphical Overviw of Tom's Father's Evaluate Dialogue

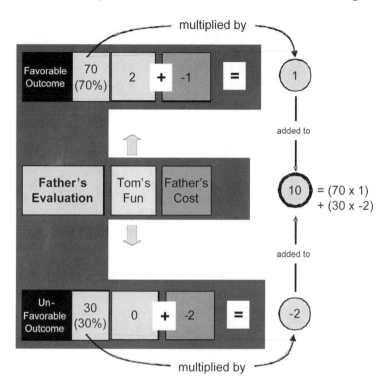

vorable" outcome occurring. (So a 30 percent chance is 30 chances out of 100.)

Step 5: Add the results of Step 3 and Step 4 to get the *value weighted by chance*.

As illustrated in Exhibit 9.5, the value weighted by chance scores for Tom are −20 for the party in the park choice and −100 for the arcade party choice. For Tom's father, the value weighted by chance scores are 10 and −100 for the park party and the arcade party, respectively.

To complete the Evaluate Dialogue, Tom and his father need to check to make sure they have addressed all of the issues, concerns, and questions raised during the Information Dialogue and understand the value story underlying the "best" choice.

Exhibit 9.6 graphically illustrates the results of Tom's father's evaluation of the "best" choice, having the "birthday party in the park on Saturday, but go to the arcade if it rains."

Applying Decision Equity with the "It Depends" Clause

For Tom and his father to apply decision equity to the evaluation, then they would apply the decision equity split they agreed to in the Value Dialogue in the previous chapter. During their Value Dialogue, they agreed to use 40 percent (or 0.40) decision equity for Tom and the remaining 60 percent (or 0.60) decision equity for Tom's father. Using the decision scorecard in Exhibit 9.5 and applying that decision equity split to Tom's and Tom's father's values weighted by chance scores for the "park party" results in a decision equity-based value score for the "park party" of –2.0. This is calculated as:

> Decision Equity-Based Score
> = (Tom's Value Weighted by Chance Score) multiplied by
>   (Tom's Decision Equity) added to
>   (Tom's Father's Value Weighted by Chance Score)
>   multiplied by (Tom's Father's Decision Equity)
> = ((–20) × (.40)) + ((10) × (.60))
> = –8.00 + 6.00
> = –2.00

The decision equity-based value score for the second choice of having an "arcade party" is –100.00.

For the Mathematically Savvy and Adventurous

The overall set of approaches to valuing decisions and outcomes we have presented has been simplified to the extent that we can simplify it and keep the approach sound. Here is an improvement that can be made to improve the rigor of the evaluation.

Apply Weights to the Value Types

Assumed in the evaluation approach is that each value type has equal weight. That is, one point of enjoyment is equal in value to one point of any other value type. While this assumption makes the mathematics simple, one can argue that an individual values some value types more than others. You can adjust the weights of the value types by creating coefficients for each value type. The approach introduced in this chapter assumes each value type has a coefficient of 1.0. As an example, for Denise's decision the value equation is:

> Value = Denise's Fun (F) + Denise's Health (H) +
>   Denise's Education (E)

where F equals the number of "fun" points and H equals the number of "health" points, and E equals the number of "education" points.

The value equation with value type coefficients becomes:

$$\text{Value} = c_1 \, F + c_2 \, H + c_3 \, E$$

Where the above definitions for F, H, and E are the same and the coefficients c_1, c_2, and c_3, represent the weights representing the personal preferences of an individual with respect to the value types.

Our intent here is merely to introduce this extension and not to develop it further since it is beyond the scope of this book.

Getting Started

Whew! Did that seem like a lot of work? Actually, once you get comfortable setting up decision scorecards, you'll find these discussions are pretty straightforward and yet very illuminating. The key here is not to make this too mechanical. Sticking with Approach 1, which does not use numbers and mathematics, is fine if that works for you and your child. If you decide to use a numerical approach (Approaches 2, 3, or 4), make sure you are having the dialogue and understand both your child's and your value scores. The numbers are only helpful if you understand the thoughts behind them.

If you are having difficulties with the "It Depends" Clause and dealing with uncertainties, don't start there. Rather use the decision scorecard design illustrated in Exhibit 9.3 as Denise and her mother did. You'll see both your and your child's decision-making capability improve immensely even if you never get around to the decision scorecards using the "It Depends" Clause and uncertainties.

Think about a decision you have recently made or better yet, one you are currently contemplating. Create a decision scorecard and fill it out for yourself. Get comfortable with the use of the 3-Point Scoring System in Exhibit 9.1 and using decision scorecards before you introduce these concepts to your children.

When introducing these concepts to your child first explain the 3-Point Scoring System and make sure they understand that they need to focus on the language rather than the numbers. The numbers are the result of finding the language that most closely represents their perception of value. For example, from the perspective of fun and enjoyment, having an ice cream cone is probably "desirable, but no big deal" and therefore scores a value of positive 1.

Once you and your child feel confident using the 3-Point Scoring System, then begin to try some simple decision scorecards.

As always, don't forget to take advantage of the characters introduced at the end of Chapter 5 (Claire Smart-Choice, Alan the Analyzer, Debra Detail, Frieda Fun Loving, Skip the Quick, and Timothy Timid) for explaining concerns you may have with your child's initial attempts at the Evaluate Dialogue and other dialogues discussed in these chapters. Statements like, "Remember Alan the Analyzer? Sometimes he really gets stuck making the math too complicated. Let's not be like that." By using the characters in your explanation we hope to create a more vivid image for your child, making your guidance easier to follow and remember.

We've said it for each FIVE-to-Decide Dialogue. Practice is required. Practice will first make you proficient and then later efficient.

Evaluate Dialogue Summary

The Evaluate Dialogue is intended to:

1. Create an understanding of the *value story* associated with each decision choice both from the child's perspective and the parent's perspective. Determine whether a best choice is revealed based on the discussion and the value scores (if applied) of the decision choices.

If Value Scoring is used:

1. Establish a value score for each type of value identified in the Value Dialogue for both the child and the parent and for each decision choice. Using a decision scorecard is recommended to keep track of the scores as you assess them.

2. Calculate a total value score for each decision choice for both the child and the parent. If you are applying the "It Depends" Clause, you will need to calculate a *value weighted by chance* total score for each choice.

A high-quality Evaluate Dialogue accomplishes four goals:

1. Truly translates both the child's and the parent's values and preferences for each decision choice;

2. Enables the child and the parent to understand each other's values and preferences for each decision choice;

3. Feels intuitively right for both child and parent; and

4. Results in the child and parent identifying a best path forward.

If your Evaluate Dialogue accomplishes these, you are ready to move on to the Decide Dialogue, creating the commitment to a path forward.

Exercises

For very young children ages 4 to 7:

1. Introduce the 3-Point Scoring System by focusing only on the language in Exhibit 9.1, not the numbers. Introduce several specific events or activities and have your child label (value) each with the language in Exhibit 9.1. (For example, is eating an ice cream cone "favorable, but no big deal" or "extremely favorable, not many things are more fun than that." How about a trip to see the grandparents, Disneyland, or some other event that you know they really enjoy?)

2. Write on seven separate flash cards the language provided in Exhibit 9.1 for the seven value scores. Write on another set of flash cards a set of value types you would like to discuss with your child (For example, fun and family quality time). Then create a situation and ask your child to place their value score (language only) card next to each of the value types. Discuss each valuation your child makes and have your child explain why they scored the event the way they did. Once your child provides and explains their value score, you provide your value score for the situation and explain your perspective.

3. For children comfortable with using numbers, introduce the simple decision scorecard illustrated in Exhibit 9.3.

For young children ages 8 to 11:

1. Introduce the 3-Point Scoring System by focusing initially only on the language in Exhibit 9.1, and then the numbers. Introduce several specific events or activities and have your child label (value) each with the language in Exhibit 9.1. (For example, is eating and ice cream cone "favorable, but no big deal" or "extremely favorable, not many things more fun than that." How about a trip to Disneyland?)

2. Write on seven separate flash cards the language provided in Exhibit 9.1 for the seven value scores and their corresponding

numbers. Write on another set of flash cards a set of value types you would like to discuss with your child (for example, fun and family quality time). Then create a situation and ask your child to place their value score card next to each of the value types. Discuss each valuation your child makes and have your child explain why they scored the event the way they did. Reinforce your child's focus on the language of the 3-Point Scoring System rather than the numerical scores. Once your child provides and explains their value score, you provide your value score for the situation and explain your perspective.

3. Introduce the concept of a decision scorecard as illustrated in Exhibit 9.3. Work through an example with both you and your child providing value scores. Keep your child focused on the language of the 3-Point Scoring System throughout the dialogue.

4. Whenever decision situations arise, hold the Evaluate Dialogue with your child. You can embed this into a complete FIVE-to-Decide Conversation or engage in just the Evaluate Dialogue to assist you and your child in thinking clearly about evaluating decision choices.

5. Ask your child what kinds of problems would "Alan the Analyzer" or "Skip the Quick" have with the Evaluate Dialogue? (See Chapter 5 for a description of Alan the Analyzer and Skip the Quick.) Follow by asking what your child's advice would be to help Alan the Analyzer or Skip the Quick do a better job with the Evaluate Dialogue.

For pre-teen and teenagers ages 12 to 15:

1. Introduce the 3-Point Scoring System. Explain the need, initially, to keep the focus on the language and not the numbers until the value-scoring becomes natural. Create an event or situation and have your child identify the relevant value types and value-score the event/situation for each value type. You provide your value scores after your child has completed their scoring. Discuss the differences in point of view and preference for situations where your and your child's value scores differ.

2. Introduce the concept of a decision scorecard as illustrated in Exhibit 9.3. Work through an example with both you and your teen providing value scores. Keep your teen focused on

the language of the 3-Point Scoring System throughout the dialogue.

3. Introduce a decision scorecard that addresses uncertainty as in Exhibit 9.5. You may want to show your teen a completed one for an introduction before attempting to create one together.

4. Whenever decision situations arise, hold the Evaluate Dialogue with your teen. You can embed this into a complete FIVE-to-Decide Conversation or engage in just the Evaluate Dialogue to assist you and your teen in thinking clearly about evaluating decision choices.

5. Ask your child what kinds of problems would "Alan the Analyzer" or "Skip the Quick" have with the Evaluate Dialogue? (See Chapter 5 for a description of Alan the Analyzer and Skip the Quick.) Follow by asking what your child's advice would be to help Alan the Analyzer or Skip the Quick do a better job with the Evaluate Dialogue.

For teenagers and young adults 16 and older:

1. Use the Exercises 1 through 5 in this chapter for pre-teens and teenagers.

2. Ask your child about a recent decision he or she made and have him or her reflect on how the concepts of the Evaluate Dialogue could have been incorporated.

The Evaluate Dialogue Guide

"Let's do the math to find the best path."

Objective

This dialogue pulls it all together. After value-scoring each alternative, you need to check and ensure that the issues and concerns raised during the Information Dialogue have been addressed in either: (1) the alternatives; (2) the information; or, (3) the values associated with the decision. Given mutual (child and parent) satisfaction with the quality of the previous dialogues, the essence of this dialogue is to evaluate each of the alternatives and understand why the highest scoring alternative(s) is preferred to all other alternatives—the "value story". Ultimately, this dialogue must answer the question, "Is there one alternative that is clearly the best choice?"

Step-by-Step Dialogue Guide

Step 1: Value-Score Each Choice (Applying the "It Depends" Clause if Required)—

(a) *Parent: "What do we do in the Evaluate Dialogue?"*

Child: (with parental coaching as needed), "Let's do the math to find the best path."

Parent: "That's right. We're ready to do our value-scoring. Which choice (alternative) would you like to start with?" Child selects an alternative and then child and parent score each value type for the selected alternative by first recalling/determining whether the "It Depends" Clause is needed and then assessing a score. Remember to assess the score from the perspective of the individual or individuals associated with the score as determined during the Value Dialogue. Example: Child scores, from the child's perspective, the value type "fun" under the situation of "no rain at the party" as a "2" and the parent, considering the child's perspective, also scores it as a "2", indicating agreement with the child that the child will enjoy the event to the degree represented by a value-score of "2". (See the Three-Point Scoring System on page 123.)

(b) *Parent: "Great. Now let's score all of the other alternatives."* Parent and child score all other alternatives, discussing their rationales as they proceed alternative by alternative. If during the discussion either the parent or child realizes a critical value type is missing, add the value type and assess value scores for each of the alternatives.

Step 2: Review "Information Needs" List and Make Sure All Information Needs Have Been Addressed—

Parent: "Let's double check to make sure we have considered all of the issues, concerns, and questions we raised in the Information Dialogue and that they were addressed at some point either in the choices we constructed, or as an assumption or uncertainty, or in the values." Go back to the issues/concerns/questions dialogue and determine if you (child and parent) are mutually satisfied that each issue/concern/question was dealt with appropriately. As required, make adjustments to the results of the previous dialogues until both the child and the parent are satisfied that all issues/concerns/questions have been addressed appropriately.

Step 3: Calculate Value Weighted by Chance (Calculate Decision Equity-Based Score If Applying Decision Equity)—

(a) *Parent: "Now, let's add up the scores for each alternative."* Child and parent add the value scores for each alternative. If you applied the "It Depends" Clause, then each alternative will have a total score for the "Favorable Outcome" and a second, separate total score for the "Unfavorable Outcome". Follow the steps outlined in Chapter 9 in the section entitled "Value Weighted by Chance Calculation" to calculate a "value weighted by chance" score for each alternative. *Optional—*If you are applying decision equity-based scores, then follow the steps outlined in Chapter 9 in the section entitled "Evaluate Approach 3: Using Decision Equity" to calculate a single, decision-equity based score for each alternative.

(b) *Parent: "Is there one alternative that is obviously the 'best' choice?"* Based on the total scores (or decision equity-based score), there may be one alternative that is clearly the best choice given both the parent and child have this alternative as the highest valued choice. However, in other cases there may be a tie for best alternative or the parent and child may have scores that indicate different "best" alternatives.

Step 4: Compare and Contrast Evaluations Across Choices to Understand and Summarize the Value Story–

(a) *Parent: "Which alternative(s) do you think is the 'best'?"* Child identifies which alternative(s) she believes is the "best" choice based on the child's scorecard and provides a rationale. Parent follows by identifying which alternative(s) parent believes is best based on parent's scorecard and provides her rationale. The dialogue should go beyond what the scores are and into the perspectives leading to the value scores. Parent should seek to understand before critiquing or offering guidance. Example: "I agree that . . . but did you consider . . ."

(b) *Parent: "In summary, what is the value story of this decision?"* Child attempts to tell the essence of why the "best" alternative is best. Parent provides her perspective after child has attempted to summarize the value story. Ex: Staying home with the family on Saturday appears to be best because of how we value "family quality time".

Step 5: Quick Check: Do You Understand Why the Highest Value Alternative is the Best Choice? Are You Confident You Have Identified the "Best" Choice?–

Parent: "Do we understand why the highest value alternative(s) is the best choice? Are we confident that we have identified the best choice(s)? Starting with the child's perspective, the child and parent have a discussion on how well they have dealt with valuing the decision choices. Do the results make sense? Are the results consistent with your intuition? Revisit any aspect of the Evaluate Dialogue or any previous dialogue that doesn't feel right.

Simple Three-Point Scoring System

Description	Score	Interpretation
High-Positive	3	Very, very desirable (good); extremely desirable (good); few things better than this
Medium-Positive	2	Very desirable (good); but not extremely desirable (good)
Low-Positive	1	Desirable (good); but no big deal
Neutral-Indifference	0	Neither desirable (good) nor undesirable (bad)
Low-Negative	−1	Undesirable (bad); but not a big deal
Medium-Negative	−2	Very undesirable (bad); but not extremely undesirable (bad)
High-Negative	−3	Very, very undesirable (bad); extremely undesirable (bad); few things worse than this

Troubleshooting Guide—Frequently Encountered Sources of Difficulty

	Issue	Suggestion
1	We added the scores and all of the alternatives resulted in about the same total scores. There is no clear "best" choice.	Revisit the Focus Dialogue. Did you really define significantly different alternatives? If not, reconsider the alternatives list. Also, revisit the results of the Value and Evaluate Dialogues. Did you make clear distinctions in scoring the various alternatives? Did you include all of the value types that are material to the alternatives?
2	One alternative looks extremely good under the "favorable outcome" but looks very bad under the "unfavorable outcome". It seems risky going with that alternative as the "best" choice.	You are right! An alternative with that type of value score is risky. However, if you applied the "It Depends" Clause and assessed the chances of a "favorable outcome", then you have accounted for the risk and uncertainty, in the choice. In the Decide Dialogue (next step) we will address this issue by determining if it is time to make the decision or see if we should wait to get more information on the critical uncertainty driving the broad range in the value score.
3	One value type (example- money) is the real driver of the decision, yet the total value score seems to give an equal weight to each of the value types. It seems like the total value score is distorted by all these other less important measures.	If one of the value types is significantly more important than all of the other value types, then use only that single value type in the Value and Evaluate Dialogues.

Evaluate Dialogue Traps To Avoid

1. **Neglecting a Key Issue or Concern**—Not addressing a nagging issue or concern for any reason is a mistake. If something feels off in the discussion, stop and try to address it head on. Remember, you have three ways to deal with issues or concerns including: (a) building it into the alternatives; (b) making an assumption about the issue or if it is an uncertainty, splitting it into a favorable outcome and an unfavorable outcome; and (c) building it into the value scores. Trust your intuition.

2. **Reducing the Decision to Numbers**—The numbers enable us to focus our conversation, but the numbers alone won't provide us the insight as to why one alternative is better than another. Go beyond the numbers and make sure you understand why an alternative is a favored choice.

3. **Parental Browbeating**—The parent asking the questions and ultimately answering the questions throughout the course of the dialogue, not listening and appropriately responding to the verbal and non-verbal cues of the child.

4. **Hurrying**—Either the parent or the child pushing the discussion faster than is appropriate, significantly reducing the quality of the discussion. This is especially problematic for the first few times you are having a decision-making conversation. Speed will come later as both the parent and child become more skilled in the process.

5. **Advocacy**—The parent or the child is approaching the discussion from that of an advocate for a particular decision definition, decision alternative (choice), or solution as opposed to approaching the discussion from that of a learning and discovery frame. This can lead to solving the wrong problem.

The Decide Dialogue:
"Choose the best thing to do,
and keep the promise true."

Mother: *Here is the situation. We're going to decide on how you should best use your free time. You did a nice job of summarizing the value story. Let me try to put it in my own words and see if you agree. We considered three choices: (1) you play on the after-school soccer team and stay up later on weekdays to do your homework with no TV watching and spend more time on homework on weekends; (2) you do not play on the after-school soccer team and spend more time on homework during the week and have more free time on the weekend; and, (3) continue with your current activities and schedule. When we evaluated these three choices we considered your enjoyment, your health, and your education. We both scored the choice of playing on the soccer team the highest in value and the reason for this was the exercise. We disagreed a little on the impact on your grades from playing on the team. But the bottom line is we both believe that playing on the after school team is the best choice. How did I do? Do you agree with all of that?*

Denise: *Yes, that's about it.*

Mother: *We'll make the decision based on what we think is right. It has to feel right in our minds and hearts.*

Denise: *Okay, so let's decide.*

The Decide Dialogue is the point at which we *make* the decision—if we are truly ready to commit. A decision is a commitment of something of value (usually time and effort or a physical asset, such as money). A decision is a commitment in that an explicit course of action is chosen, implying other potential courses of action are forgone. All of the previous chapter dialogues have been leading to this point of the process. As we will detail, making the decision ultimately requires the alignment of

> *Claire's Comment:*
> The Decide Dialogue is where you have to connect with your mind and heart. It's not about numbers here. You need to feel confident that the best choice is the *best* choice. This can be a tough discussion because both the parent and the child really need to tell each other what they feel is right and why. You really have to listen carefully to each other. If you are not ready to decide, understand why and agree on how to get to the decision—the commitment.

mind (logical reasoning) and heart (reasoning through feelings) to a choice. The Decide Dialogue concludes in one of three results: (1) the commitment to a choice; (2) a reconsideration of one or more of the previous dialogues; or, (3) the decision to wait for some additional information before making a commitment.

Creating Real Commitment Is No Small Accomplishment

The FIVE-to-Decide Conversation is designed to create commitment, which is no small accomplishment. For individuals to get to a point of commitment it usually requires the individual to evolve through at least four stages as depicted in Exhibit 10.1. It is important to realize that creating true commitment is a process. Other than for cases of emergencies and crises where there is no time to hesitate, individuals need to go through each of the stages of awareness, comprehension, and endorsement before they can truly commit. Think through the FIVE-to-Decide approach and determine where the four stages to commitment occur.

Matters of the Mind and Heart

It is generally believed that there are two different but complementary modes of thinking—*left-brain thinking* and *right-brain thinking*. *Left-brain thinking* is characterized as logical, analytical, rational, sequential, objective and is driven from a "sum of the parts" perspective. In contrast, *right-brain thinking* is characterized as intuitive, subjective, synthesizing, holistic and is driven from a "consider the whole" perspective. Individuals usually have a tendency to favor

Exhibit 10.1: The Four Stages to Commitment

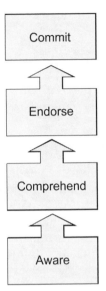

Stage 4: Commit—Accepting a personal role in the pursuit of a course of action including the risks, responsibilities, accountabilities, and consequences of that acceptance. This includes the personal commitment of resources to pursue a course of action—a *decision*.

Stage 3: Endorse—Support for a particular course of action with no personal stake in the action or ultimate outcome.

Stage 2: Comprehend—Understanding of the issues and concerns and the potential courses of action with their respective costs, risks, and benefits.

Stage 1: Aware—Recognition of the need and urgency for some, as yet unclear, course of action to pursue.

one or the other of these modes, though some individuals seem to easily integrate the two modes of thinking.

The FIVE-to-Decide steps from the Focus through the Evaluate dialogues are oriented primarily as left-brain thinking. It is in the Decide Dialogue that we must think holistically and bring the entire set of dialogues together and give them a good top-down, holistic scrubbing.

Once you understand the value story resulting from the Evaluate Dialogue, you must ask yourself, "Does this feel intuitively right?" In your "heart of hearts" is it clear that one choice stands out as "best" and are you (parent and child) compelled to commit to that choice. If you are not compelled, you need to understand why not! In answering the "why not" question, be prepared to have the most open and honest dialogue with your child on the issues at hand. Be prepared to listen very carefully to your child, for if anything important has been unsaid, this will be the best opportunity to reveal it and resolve any outstanding issues or concerns.

Sleep on It

Folk wisdom suggests that having a night's rest, or "sleeping on it" helps to make good decisions. Recent research has supported this conclusion by claiming that the unconscious mind is better at accounting and weighing complex options than the conscious mind is. It is likely that you have experienced the sense of a clearer mind on an issue after a good night's sleep. Consequently, you might find it "good practice" for tough decisions to have the FIVE-to-Decide Conversation up through the Evaluate Dialogue and to postpone the Decide Dialogue until the next day. This will allow you and your child to revisit the results of each of the dialogues with a fresh mind and to either confirm the results or make modifications you deem appropriate prior to making the decision.

"Choose the best thing to do, and keep the promise true"

The bottom line here is that the Decide Dialogue is where the child and parent "choose the best thing to do, and keep the promise true." The promise is the commitment to a choice, a course of action, with all of its requisite commitments of resources (time, effort, money, or something else of value to the child or parent.). The accountability of this commitment resides between the child and the parent. The child is accountable for taking all of the actions and commitment of resources required to fulfill their role in pursuing the "best" choice and the parent is accountable for the same in their role given the parent has an active role in implementing the decision.

The parent also has a second crucial role. And that is to remove, to the extent possible, any hurdles or roadblocks the child may have in fulfilling their commitments determined by the decision. This could include: relaxing time commitments for homework on a given day or minimizing family chores over a specific time period.

The essence of the Decide Dialogue is contained in three simple steps:

1. Understand/Confirm (both the child and the parent) the value story for each choice and understand why one choice is "best" from the perspective of value.
2. Answer (both the child and parent) the question, "Does the 'best' choice make sense?" for *both* the mind and the heart. If the "best" choice does make sense, then you should be ready to commit to the "best" choice. If not, then you need to understand why not.
3. Make the commitment (both the child and the parent), reconsider, or wait. If you can't make the connection between mind and heart and ultimately can't make the commitment to a choice, then you will need to understand why. Resolving why you can't make the commitment may require as little as a minor change in the evaluation section or as much as establishing an entire new focus and decision to consider. You may

determine that you need to wait for some additional information prior to making the decision and committing the requisite resources to fulfill the commitment.

Let's return to Denise and her mother and the decision regarding Denise's free time. At the beginning of this chapter they had reached an understanding of the value story.

Mother: Does playing on the after school soccer team seem to be the best choice for your mind and heart?

Denise: Absolutely.

DON'T! **Mother:** That's good. I have to admit, I still feel a little uneasy over this. I'm still concerned about your grades and you spending enough time on your school work. I'm worried that you won't have the energy to devote to your school work.

Denise: What doesn't feel right about it? What are you thinking about?

Mother: I trust that you will try to make it work. I just think it will be tough for you to juggle all of this.

> Don't be like Timothy Timid:
> • How might Timothy Timid shy away from this discussion and not express his concerns as we get close to making a decision?
> • How would you help Timothy open up and express his opinion on the value story or his concerns at this point in the FIVE-to-Decide Conversation?
> • Is there a little Timothy Timid in you or your child?

Denise: Mom, listen. I promise I will let you know if I am slipping a little at school. I'll give you my teachers' e-mail addresses and you can keep in touch with them. Will that help? Some of my friends' moms are doing that.

Mother: That's a good idea. That would help. I'm really proud of how you are thinking about all of this!

Denise: I just think playing on the after school soccer team is a good thing to do and that I *can* balance everything.

Mother: Okay. It feels right to me. Are you ready to commit with your mind and your heart?

Denise: Yes. I'll call Cindy and tell her I'm going out for the team.

Mother: That's great. Denise, that was a really good conversation. You're doing the right thing. I hope you really enjoy playing on the team.

Exhibit 10.2 illustrates the essence of the Decide Dialogue, simultaneously weighing both the mind and heart at the time of making the commitment to a choice.

Exhibit 10.2 The Essence of the Decide Dialogue: Balancing Commitment of the Mind and Heart

Tom's Birthday Party Decision—The Decide Dialogue

Father: What do we do in the Decide Dialogue?

Tom: Choose the best thing to do, and keep the promise true.

Father That's right. You did a good job summarizing the value story. Let me try to say it in my own words. We both scored having your party in the park as the best choice. And the real value is having the option to go to the arcade if it rains. It's a win-win whether it rains or not. That's what it boils down to. Does that sound right?

Tom: It does.

Father: But does that feel right? Is there anything that makes you question whether this is really the best choice?

Tom: I have no doubt. I'm completely convinced.

Father: I am too. I think we're ready to decide. Let's do it. Let's go for the park party and I'll make a reservation at the arcade.

Tom: I'll call all of my friends and let them know the plan.

Father: You did a great job on this. I think we had a great conversation.

Tom: I do, too. Thanks Dad!

Getting Started

In some respects, this may be the most natural of the dialogues in the FIVE-to-Decide approach. Chances are, you have been having Decide dialogues with your children for sometime. The difference here is that if you have followed the FIVE-to-Decide approach, you and your child will be very prepared to have an efficient and effective dialogue that will lead to a decision—a true commitment.

For yourself, think back to a recent difficult decision you have made. Did the decision feel right for both your mind and heart? If not, why not? Think about decisions you have made in the past under circumstances that your heart probably was not aligned with the decision. In those situations, did you really commit to a course of action? Did you really follow through with the commitment? Now, consider the situation where you followed your heart in making a decision even though logically it seemed like your choice was the wrong thing to do. What happened in that situation or situations? Did the decision stick?

Many commitments in life die slow deaths due to neglect. Many business managers are good at agreeing to do something they are not committed to do, knowing all along that if they just ignore it time and events will overtake the situation and all will be forgotten—most importantly their personal commitment. As a parent, you need to demonstrate for your children the leadership associated with decision making with the hope that your role modeling will positively influence your child's skills and behaviors in decision making. The Decide Dialogue is a good platform for demonstrating the leadership skills of decision making: creativity, willingness to consider new possibilities, and little advocacy for any given choice until after the decision is made.

For your child, explain the concept of mind (logical reasoning) versus heart (reasoning through feelings) and the importance of aligning your mind and heart to a commitment. Begin to nurture the ability of you and your child to discuss both matters of the mind and heart. At this point you and your child probably have a tendency to discuss things from predominantly one perspective or the other, but not both. Your goal should be to be an effective communicator with your child for both matters of the mind and heart. In doing so, you will be a wonderful role model for your child's overall development and providing your child skills that will benefit them for a lifetime.

One last time, don't forget to take advantage of the characters introduced at the end of Chapter 5 (Claire Smart-Choice, Alan the Analyzer, Debra Detail, Frieda Fun Loving, Skip the Quick, and Timothy Timid) for explaining concerns you may have with your child's initial attempts at the Decide Dialogue and other dialogues discussed in these chapters. Statements like, "Remember Timothy Timid? Sometimes he really has a hard time telling what he thinks and feels. Let's not be like that." By using the characters in your explanation we hope to create a more vivid image for your child, making your guidance easier to follow and remember.

Decide Dialogue Summary

The Decide Dialogue is intended to:

1. Ensure that both the child and the parent understand the value story for each choice and understand why one choice is "best" from the perspective of value.

2. Answer the question, "Does the 'best' choice make sense?" for *both* the mind and the heart. The parent and the child will be ready to commit to a choice only after both the child and the parent are resolved in both mind and heart for a specific choice.

3. Either: (a) make the decision, the commitment to a choice and commit the requisite resources to fulfill the commitment; (b) reconsider the decision by taking the time to address the reasons of why you can't truly commit at this time; or, (c) wait for the additional important information you need to have prior to making the decision.

A high-quality Decide Dialogue accomplishes two goals:

1. Creates an inner peace for both the child and the parent regarding the "best" choice (course of action) for the situation and decision addressed in the FIVE-to-Decide Conversation; and,

2. Establishes the agreement and commitment of both the parent and the child to the course of action associated with the "best" choice within the required time frame.

Congratulations! You have completed the FIVE-to-Decide approach to decision making.

Exercises

For very young children ages 4 to 7:

1. Discuss with your child that making a decision is making a promise to do something. Discuss with them some recent decisions you have made on your child's behalf and explain what the implicit promises were in those decisions.

2. Ask your child about recent choices they have made (e.g., what they ordered in a recent trip to a restaurant or fast food provider) and discuss what choices they had forgone by mak-

ing their choice (e.g., ordering a hamburger meant that they couldn't have pasta).

3. For children comfortable with using numbers, go back to an example you worked through using the scoring system in Chapter 9 and discuss making a decision based on that evaluation. Discuss how they *feel* about the results of the evaluation. Does it *feel* right? Why or why not?

For young children ages 8 to 11:

1. Discuss with your child that making a decision is making a promise to do something. Discuss with them some recent decisions they have made and discuss what the implicit promises were in those decisions.

2. Discuss with your child the nature of creating commitment and in doing so and to the extent possible, use the concepts of the *four stages of commitment* illustrated in Exhibit 10.1.

3. Discuss with your child the difference between matters of the mind (logical reasoning) and matters of the heart (reasoning through feelings). Discuss how in decision making that we really need to do both and that aligning the mind and heart, to the extent we can, is a necessary part of making decisions and ensuring commitment.

4. Ask your child to discuss some of their recent decisions from the perspective of matters of the mind and matters of the heart. Ask your child to assess whether they had resolved both perspectives before making the decision. If they had not, what happened to the commitment?

5. Whenever decision situations arise, hold the Decide Dialogue with your child. You can embed this into a complete FIVE-to-Decide Conversation or engage in just the Decide Dialogue to assist you and your child in thinking clearly about making decisions.

6. Ask your child what kinds of problems would "Timothy Timid" have with the Decide Dialogue? (See Chapter 5 for a description of Timothy Timid.) Follow by asking what your child's advice would be to help Timothy Timid do a better job with the Decide Dialogue.

For pre-teen and teenagers ages 12 to 15:

1. Discuss with your teenager that making a decision is making a promise to do something. Discuss with them some recent decisions they have made and discuss what the implicit promises were in those decisions.

2. Discuss with your teenager the nature of creating commitment and in doing so, use the concepts of the *four stages of commitment* illustrated in Exhibit 10.1.

3. Discuss with your teenager the difference between matters of the mind (logical reasoning) and matters of the heart (reasoning through feelings). Discuss how in decision making that we really need to do both and that aligning the mind and heart, to the extent we can, is a necessary part of making decisions and ensuring commitment.

4. Ask your teenager to discuss some of their recent decisions from the perspective of matters of the mind and matters of the heart. Ask your teenager to assess whether they had resolved both perspectives before making the decision. If they had not, what happened to the commitment?

5. Discuss the issue of peer pressure at school and how it influences their *feelings* in decision making. Discuss the leadership characteristics of being a good decision maker (creativity, willingness to consider new possibilities, and low advocacy for any given choice until after the decision is made) and the importance, now and in the future, of aspiring to these characteristics and behavior.

6. Whenever decision situations arise, hold the Decide Dialogue with your teenager. You can embed this into a complete FIVE-to-Decide Conversation or engage in just the Decide Dialogue to assist you and your teenager in thinking clearly about making decisions.

For teenagers and young adults 16 and older:

1. Use the exercises 1 through 6 listed above for pre-teen and teenagers.

2. Make an agreement with your young adult about always checking and discussing matters of the mind and heart in future decision making.

The Decide Dialogue Guide

"Choose the best thing to do, and keep the promise true."

Objective

After establishing a mutual understanding and agreement on the "value story" of the decision, the parent and child need to determine whether they are: (1) ready to make the decision; (2) need to reconsider the decision; or, (3) need to wait for additional information before making the decision.

Step-by-Step Dialogue Guide

Step 1: Understand/Confirm the Value Story for the Decision—

Parent: "What do we do in the Decide Dialogue?"
Child: (with parental coaching as needed), "Choose the best thing to do, and keep the promise true."
Parent: "Let me summarize the value story. (Insert summary of value story stated.) Does that sound right to you?" Parent summarizes the value story for the child in an attempt to both confirm the value story and ensure there is mutual agreement on the value story. If there is not agreement, parent and child should seek to understand the source of the disagreement and make adjustments wherever they are needed in previous dialogues to reach an agreement.

Step 2: Does the Best Choice Make Sense for the Mind and Heart?-

The steps in the FIVE-to-Decide approach will drive the decision conversation to a logical "best" choice—a matter of the mind. But does that "best" choice feel right?—a matter of the heart. True commitment to action usually requires both agreement between mind and heart. The intent of this step is primarily to check to determine whether the "best" choice feels right for both the child and parent. *Parent: "Does (insert statement of 'best' choice) feel right to you?"* Parent carefully listens to how the child feels about the "best" choice. The child may reveal new insights about their issues and concerns that need to be dealt with before reaching a commitment to an alternative. Be prepared to revisit and possibly revise previous step dialogues to address the issue of "feeling right". Parent provides their perspective on how they feel about the best choice after the child has offered their perspective.

Step 3: Commit, Reconsider, or Wait?—

Parent: "Are you ready to commit to (insert statement of best choice)?" Given the child and the parent agree, in mind and heart, on the "best" choice, then both the child and parent should be prepared and motivated to commit to the "best" choice and its requisite actions to fulfill the commitment. Child and parent verbally commit to the best choice. For complex decisions you may consider "sleeping on it" prior to making the decision.

If the child and parent have not reached an agreement, in mind and heart, on the "best" choice, then the child and parent must determine whether they need to reconsider and revise any of the previous dialogue steps (Focus, Information, Value, or Evaluate). For decisions where the Information Dialogue was difficult and unsatisfying (Ex: the assumptions were not "good assumptions" or the "chances in 100" for a favorable outcome was very difficult to assess (or parent and child significantly disagreed on the number of chances) then the parent and child should consider postponing the decision until they can improve their "state of information" by confirming assumptions or getting improved assessments of an uncertainty. The caveat in postponing the decision is that you may lose some of your choices if you wait too long. (Ex: Cannot apply to your favorite university because you missed the application deadline.)

Troubleshooting Guide—Frequently Encountered Sources of Difficulty

	Issue	Suggestion
1	We carefully followed the FIVE-to-Decide approach but it didn't lead to the choice we feel is best.	Check to determine whether there is an issue or concern that was not addressed or one that was not addressed satisfactorily. Also, check your value scores to make sure they accurately reflect your preferences and those of other individuals listed in the Value Dialogue. Revise any aspects of the dialogues that seem wrong. However, don't go back to make changes just to rationalize your beliefs about which choice is best! Ultimately, you (parent and child) must feel that the value story is correct and if that is the case, you should have sufficient motivation and commitment to proceed with a course of action consistent with the "best" choice.
2	We carefully followed the FIVE-to-Decide approach but we (parent and child) disagree on which alternative is the "best" choice.	Understand the specific details about the source of disagreement. If the focus is correct, it is very likely that the source of disagreement is in the value scores. Seek to mutually understand the thinking behind all value scores where the child and parent have different scores. If after this dialogue the child's scores and the parent's scores still indicate different "best" choices, consider applying the decision equity-based scoring discussed in Chapters 8 and 9 in order to determine the "best" choice and course of action.

Decide Dialogue Traps To Avoid

1. **Failing to Address Your Feelings**—The FIVE-to-Decide approach will drive your decision conversation to a logical conclusion; but that is not enough to create true commitment. The parent and child must also ensure that they have considered how they feel about the "best" choice. Does the "best" choice feel right? If not, why not?

2. **You Make the Decision, the Process Doesn't**—The FIVE-to-Decide approach is intended to create a comprehensive conversation between a child and a parent to *enable* the creation of sufficient commitment—both parent and child—to a decision choice and course of action. The Evaluate Dialogue does not "tell you" what to do. The Evaluate Dialogue enables a clear discussion that hopefully illuminates the underlying value story of the decision. Ultimately, you (the child and parent) must draw your own conclusions from the conversation and make the commitment to a choice.

3. **Parental Browbeating**—The parent asking the questions and ultimately answering the questions throughout the course of the dialogue, not listening and appropriately responding to the verbal and non-verbal cues of the child.

4. **Hurrying**—Either the parent or the child pushing the discussion faster than is appropriate, significantly reducing the quality of the discussion. This is especially problematic for the first few times you are having a decision-making conversation. Speed will come later as both the parent and child become more skilled in the process.

5. **Advocacy**—The parent or the child is approaching the dialogue from that of an advocate for a particular choice, biasing the discussion in ways that create a rationale for their desired choice.

Claire's Summary

For the past couple of years I have been using the FIVE-to-Decide approach in order to make many of my decisions. It's become a pretty natural tendency, and every time I need to make a decision, I use it. For simplicity's sake, I just call it the "5D."

Dr. Charette and Dr. Hagen really go into detail on the process within the book. It may come off as really complicated after reading through it, while in truth it really isn't. It's actually quite simple when you start using it. I'd like to tell you about my version of the "5D." I made a one page worksheet that a lot of my friends are using. I've provided you an example of a completed worksheet (see Exhibit 11.1) for Tom's birthday party decision at the end of this note. I think this will help you get started. My friends like it and so do Dr. Charette and Dr. Hagen, so here it is! First, carefully read my example worksheet and then read my summary below. The FIVE-to-Decide approach will make a lot more sense after you do the following steps.

Focus: "Look up, look down, then all the way around."

Focus

Don't get hung up on the decision definition. All you really want to accomplish is getting good choices on the table. In fact, I usually work back and forth a little with the decision definition and the choices. The tricky part is when you're really worried about making a wrong decision. Whenever this is the case, try to have at least one choice that will keep your options open later, like a choice that let's you test out a situation before you make a full commitment. As an example, if you're not sure whether you will like taking guitar lessons, then see if you can sign up for a couple of lessons to try it out before you commit to a full year of lessons. In the example worksheet, Tom did this by keeping his option open to go to the arcade if it started to rain at the park during his birthday party.

Information: "What makes the decision hard or tough? What information is just enough?"

Information

F I

For this step, you really have to start with what your gut feeling is. Look at the choices and ask yourself, "Why am I not sure which choice is best?" Just write down whatever comes to your mind as an issue. Usually there are one or two *real* issues or concerns you have about a decision once you give it some thought. If you feel that you have many issues, you need to try and isolate what you think are the one or two most prominent factors at the core of your concerns. This is a very important part of the whole process— digging deep to understand what is truly making the decision hard to make. Also, being honest with yourself is *very* important. And always make sure you know which issue is the biggest issue on your list. Sometimes I put a little star on that issue so I'll remember to make sure that I'm satisfied with how the issue is handled in the evaluate section before I make my decision.

After you have completed your issue list, go back and categorize your issues as either "A" for an assumption, "U" for an uncertainty, and "V" for value-related. If you're not sure in some cases, just give it your best guess on the category. You can always go back and change it later. That's true for the whole worksheet! I personally am always going back and changing things a little because as I step through the process I often think about my decision differently. Remember, assumptions should not include your wishes about the future—assumptions represent facts about the future. I usually have at most one issue I treat as an uncertainty and for the rest of the issues I make them into assumptions or treat them as value-related.

The Information Dialogue is basically just using your gut feelings to make a list of your issues. Use your head to categorize the issues as assumptions, uncertainties, or value-related. If you mark an issue as an assumption, then write down what your assumption is. If you mark an issue as an uncertainty, try to state the uncertainty in the form of a question. If you mark an issue as value-related, just note that the issue needs to be addressed in the Evaluate section.

Value: "What's 'good'? What's 'bad'? Let's ask Mom or Dad."

Value

F I V

I always thought the first part of this step was pretty easy. Just look at the choices one at a time and identify which value types are important to *you*. Then go through the list of choices a second time and think, "Which of these value types would my Mom or Dad add?" When I do it this way and show my Mom, she almost never adds another value type to my list. After you are done checking off the value types that apply to your decision, go back and write down from whose perspective.

The tricky part is that you need to check to see if you need the "It Depends" Clause. If you have marked one of your issues as uncertain, check to see whether any of the value types you checked off will need different value scores depending on the outcome of the uncertain issue. If the answer is yes—the value score will depend on the outcome of the uncertainty—then you will need to apply the "It Depends" Clause. For the issue marked as uncertain, "U," you have to write down what would be a good outcome for that uncertainty—a favorable outcome—and then also what would be a bad outcome for that uncertainty—an unfavorable outcome. For Tom, a favorable outcome was not having it rain at the park on or before his party.

Once you are clear on your definitions for a favorable outcome and an unfavorable outcome, then you need to determine what the chances are that you will end up with the favorable outcome and what the chances are that you will end up with the unfavorable outcome. Remember that these two numbers must add up to 100. Tom used the weatherman's report to conclude that there was a 30 percent chance of rain on Saturday so Tom used 30 chances in 100 for his unfavorable outcome. If you didn't mark any of your issues as uncertain, you can ignore the section on the worksheet regarding favorable and unfavorable outcomes and chances in 100.

Evaluate: "Let's do the math to find the best path."

Evaluate

F I V E

Remember that each choice within this section needs to be evaluated for each value type that you select. I've added a little comment section so I can keep track of my thoughts as I score the choices. The three-point scoring system is easy to use but you have to remember that giving a "3" or a "-3" is an unusual score because it is an extreme score. A "3" for "fun" means that there are only a few things in life that are as fun or more fun than the choice you are giving a "3". On the other hand, a "-3" means there are only a few things as bad or worse than the choice you are considering for the value type you are measuring. So most of my scores are zeroes, ones, and twos, using the plus and minus signs as the three point scoring system suggests. Remember, a minus number means it's a bad outcome for that value type. As an example, if something costs money then your wealth goes down, so you need to assign a negative number for wealth for outcomes including cost. But if you receive money for something, then your wealth goes up. Consequently, your value score should be a positive number. Ultimately, you need to go with what your feelings say is right. The scores are also in respect to someone's perspective—such as yours, or your parents.

To get the weighted score for yourself or for your parents, you have to do a little math. Let's look at Tom's example to explain this and consider his first choice of having a birthday party in the park and moving to the arcade if it rains. To get Tom's weighted score, first add up his favorable scores and you get "1". Then, add up his unfavorable scores and you get "–3". Take the "1" and multiply it by "70" (the number of chances in 100 of a favorable outcome) and you get "70". Now take "–3" and multiply it by "30" (the number of chances in 100 of an unfavorable outcome) and you get "–90". Add the "70" with the "-90" and you get "–20", Tom's weighted score for his first choice.

Once you have calculated the weighted score for each of the choices for both yourself and your parents, then you need to look at the numbers and understand what the *value story* is telling you. Why is one choice better than the others? What have you learned about the decision?

Notice that my worksheet allows you to use decision equity in the evaluation. I have it in my worksheet to be complete, but I don't always use that part of the worksheet.

Decide: *"Choose the best thing to do, and keep the promise true."*

Decide Before choosing the best decision, keep this in mind. The choice you make should not be based on your scores alone. Don't just look at the numbers and make a decision right off the bat. Make sure that your feelings have come into agreement with the numbers that are calculated. Once you check your math and understand the value story you have to ask yourself, Does this make sense? Does this feel right? Is this really the best choice? If the answer to those questions are yes, then great, go ahead and make the commitment. If not, go back and review everything starting with your focus on through the evaluation. Does it all make sense? If something doesn't feel right then change it; but, don't just rationalize things to get what you want. Be HONEST with yourself if you are going to make a change. The bottom line is if you're truly going to commit to something, you will need to come to peace with the "best" choice—and this means making a connection and agreement between your feelings and brain.

Make It Work for You

All of my friends that are using "5D" have created their own style and approach. You need to make it work for you while using the guidance that Dr. Charette and Dr. Hagen have provided. Once you feel like you really own your own approach, then this seemingly difficult process will become very natural. But like most things, it takes practice to get there.

Exhibit 11.1: Tom's Birthday Party Decision Worksheet

<table>
<tr><td rowspan="5">FOCUS</td><td colspan="2">Decision Definition</td><td colspan="2">Decision Choices</td></tr>
<tr><td>Test:</td><td>What should we do if it rains at the park?</td><td></td><td></td></tr>
<tr><td>Bigger:</td><td>Where should Tom's party be and when?</td><td>→ 1</td><td>Birthday Party in Park on Saturday; but Go to Arcade if Rain</td></tr>
<tr><td>Smaller:</td><td>Where should Tom's B-day party be?</td><td>→ 2</td><td>Birthday Party at Arcade with Laser Tag</td></tr>
<tr><td>Selected:</td><td>Where should Tom's B-day party be?</td><td>→ 3</td><td>Choice 3</td></tr>
</table>

<table>
<tr><td rowspan="5">INFORMATION</td><td colspan="2">Issues and Concerns</td><td colspan="2">Assumption / Uncertainty / Value Related</td></tr>
<tr><td>1</td><td>Will friends like arcade party as much as park party?</td><td>A</td><td>Friends like arcade party as much as park party.</td></tr>
<tr><td>2</td><td>How does Tom feel about a park party in the rain?</td><td>V</td><td>Need to address in evaluation.</td></tr>
<tr><td>3</td><td>Will it rain at the park before or during the party?</td><td>U</td><td>Will it rain at the park before or during the party?</td></tr>
<tr><td>4</td><td>There is a $50 late cancellation fee for the arcade.</td><td>V</td><td>Need to address in evaluation.</td></tr>
</table>

<table>
<tr><td rowspan="8">VALUE</td><td colspan="4">Check all Value Types that Apply and State from Whose Perspective:</td></tr>
<tr><td>X Enjoyment (Fun)   Tom's</td><td>Learning _____</td><td>Pain
X Money   Dad's Cost</td></tr>
<tr><td>Health _____</td><td>Family Quality Time _____</td><td>Personal Fulfillment</td></tr>
<tr><td>Safety _____</td><td>Charity _____</td><td>Time _____</td></tr>
<tr><td colspan="4">Decision Equity (DE): Must add to 100%</td></tr>
<tr><td colspan="4">Child: 40%   Parent(s): 60%</td></tr>
<tr><td colspan="4">Do You Need the "It Depends" Clause? If Yes, Define Outcomes and Assess Chances:</td></tr>
<tr><td colspan="2">Chances
in 100
70
Favorable Outcome
It does not rain at the park on or before the party on Saturday.</td><td colspan="2">Chances
in 100
30
Unfavorable Outcome
It rains at the park on or before the party on Saturday.</td></tr>
</table>

	Choice	Comments	Value Type / Who	Outcome	Score C	Score P
EVALUATE		If it rains, Tom thinks it will be no fun moving the party to the arcade	Tom's Fun	Favorable	2	2
				Unfavorable	-1	0
		Dad will pay arcade deposit to keep the arcade party option available. The arcade party costs more.	Dad's Cost	Favorable	-1	-1
	Birthday Party in Park on Saturday; but Go to Arcade if Rain			Unfavorable	-2	-2
				Favorable		
				Unfavorable		
				Favorable		
				Unfavorable		
		Child's Weighted Score -20 / Parent's Weighted Score 10	DE Score -2.00 Total	Favorable	1	1
				Unfavorable	-3	-2
		Tom won't have as much fun at the arcade party.	Tom's Fun	Favorable	1	1
				Unfavorable	1	1
		The arcade party is quite a bit more expensive than the park party.	Dad's Cost	Favorable	-2	-2
	Birthday Party at Arcade with Laser Tag			Unfavorable	-2	-2
				Favorable		
				Unfavorable		
				Favorable		
				Unfavorable		
		Child's Weighted Score -100 / Parent's Weighted Score -100	DE Score -100.00 Total	Favorable	-1	-1
				Unfavorable	-1	-1
				Favorable		
				Unfavorable		
				Favorable		
				Unfavorable		
	Choice 3			Favorable		
				Unfavorable		
				Favorable		
				Unfavorable		
		Child's Weighted Score 0 / Parent's Weighted Score 0	DE Score 0.00 Total	Favorable	0	0
				Unfavorable	0	0

<table>
<tr><td rowspan="2">DECIDE</td><td>Best Choice</td><td>Value Story</td></tr>
<tr><td>Have Tom's party in the park; but, go to the arcade if it rains.</td><td>Going to the park is the best choice as long as Tom and his father keep the arcade option open.</td></tr>
</table>

PART III

Putting It into Practice

The Never-Ending Conversation

The son of a friend of ours, named Patrick, is a young air force pilot serving in Korea. Throughout college, through flight training, and now out on deployment, Patrick holds regular conversations with his father, Jack. A lot of what Patrick talks with his father about are the decisions he had to make that particular day as a pilot, but also about upcoming decisions he has to make in terms of his career, personal life, and the issues of living in a different country.

Jack and Patrick have been holding these regular conversations since Patrick was in high school. Jack says back then, the conversations were more father-to-son in nature, but now they have grown into full adult-to-adult conversations. Jack says with pride that he couldn't imagine doing the things his son is doing, and how he is learning so much new from his son—a total role reversal.

Jack also likes to say how, Patrick, the decision maker of today, is not the decision maker he was just a few years ago. Part of the reason is not only Pat's increased maturity, but the fact that flight training is very centered on empowering a young pilot candidate's decision-making skills along each step in the path on becoming a fully qualified pilot. A pilot has to be able to make a tremendous number of correct decisions under both physical and mental stress, the reason being that a poor decision can harm not only themselves but many others.

At flight training, a young pilot candidate's decision-making (and, of course, flying) skills are steadily increased in a series of very deliberate, increasingly difficult, steps. Mistakes are common and expected along the way. However, each young pilot's mistakes are reviewed with their instructors, who give feedback strictly based on the pilot's performance. Pilots are expected to learn from their mistakes.

As the training increases in difficulty, the nature of any mistake made is increasingly used to decide who moves on in training. Preventable or repeated mistakes in decision making are not acceptable, for each step in training brings a faster, more powerful and more complex aircraft to fly, and with it, a decrease in the time to decide and to react. Being able to make decisions calmly under what is called "task saturation" is the hallmark of a competent pilot.

We can remember Jack telling us how, at each new stage of training, his son would discuss about how hard the whole thing was, occasionally asking how was it possible for anyone to learn everything that needed to be learned and manage all the tasks that needed to be managed in such a short amount of time. Patrick also discussed with his dad how would he react in an emergency— would he be up to it? Jack and Patrick held many midnight conversations during flight school.

Well, Patrick not only survived, but thrived throughout his flight training experience, graduating near the top of his class. And in the emergencies that Patrick has faced, he made the correct decisions, which is what his training had taught him to do.

Another friend of ours, George, has a young daughter, Brianne, working in Washington, DC, for the government in a high-profile job. Brianne's dad also holds regular conversations with his daughter on the decisions she has or has to make, similar to what Jack does with his son. Other friends of ours also hold regular conversations with their adult children. What is interesting is in our conversations with our friends is they all agree that, looking back, their current relationship with their children is largely based on the principles of good decision making they taught their children growing up. As Jack and George related to us, if you teach your children good decision-making skills, then they will *want* to talk to you as they grow into adults.

Getting Started

Jack, George, and others who have such wonderful relationships with their children do not have formal educations in decision making. But they decided long ago that they had to learn how to make better decisions so that they could in turn teach their children. They admit they were not perfect at it and that they made plenty of mistakes along the way. It all worked out in the end, but they said that it would have been easier if something—like FIVE-to-Decide—had been available back then.

We're flattered by the compliment. However, we also asked our friends if in the process of teaching themselves decision making, did the learning process cause them to change their own behavior? They all admitted that this was the case—to be a good decision maker, they said, you have to change something in yourself. Before learning a more disciplined approach to decision making, our friends said that they tended to make decisions in a fairly ad hoc manner. It took some conscious effort and commitment on their part to change how they approached making decisions. It was hard and a little awkward in the beginning, but the process got easier over time.

What Jack, George, and others did without realizing it was that they were empowering their children's decision making. They consciously went out of their way to first improve their children's capability to make better decisions, and then as the children matured, increasingly gave them more say in making their own decisions as well as the responsibility for the consequences. But, as we said, each of our friends first had to change how they went about making decisions themselves, which is your first step too.

Parents: Teaching Yourself Decision Making

All change follows three mutually reinforcing stages. The first stage is understanding what you need to do—or maybe better stated—what do you need to do differently? Do you currently make decisions quickly, without reflection? Do you choose the first alternative that satisfies your criterion instead of weighing each alternative available? If so, you are like most of us who have never been taught good decision making. Look at how you make decisions and compare them to the FIVE-to-Decide approach described in this book. What needs to change?

The second stage is commitment. Once you are aware of what you need to change, you need to commit to making that change stick. We think that this commitment is not trivial, but it is not insurmountable either. We don't expect you to become an expert decision maker before focusing on your kids. You are going to learn together and from each other. You are also going to increase your awareness and understanding of what you need to improve in your own decision making.

The third and last stage is practice, practice, practice. We all learn by doing—not by reading books. Reading a parenting book does not make you a parent. Books like this can help guide you, but change in your and your children's current decision habits will only happen when you have practiced enough so that new decision-making habits are created.

Think about what decision-making aspects you need to do more—for example, working on the focus of the decision is critical to making a good decision and is something even we as professional decision consultants have to work on constantly. Then think about what decision-making aspects you need to do less—maybe jumping to a decision without thinking through the relevant information readily available to make an informed decision. If either of these characteristics isn't obvious, just think of the last time you said to yourself, "It seemed like a good idea at the time." This will give you some clues on what and where you need to improve.

You most likely already have lots of other good decision skills that you want to keep. We encourage you to build on those as you add or subtract those decision-making behaviors that need to be changed.

Also, don't forget that we have to do the same things that you do. Our children, for example, do not care that we help executives make decisions, teach classes on it, or have written books on the subject. None of those makes our own children better decision makers. We may be more experienced in decision making than you, but we have to practice diligently with our own children all the time as well.

Parents: Teaching Your Children

In Chapter 5, we talked about how to create a satisfying conversation. We encourage you to re-read that chapter as you determine which decision-making habits you may need to change or reinforce. On top of these good rules for holding a conversation, you may want to consider a few additional ideas on teaching your child decision making.

First, think about creating a decision-making review routine, especially for your children as they enter school. A friend of ours reviews the day's decisions with each of her four girls every night before bedtime. It gives our friend insight into what is bothering her children without being overly inquisitive or to her teenagers, "prying." It is something she did when her girls started kindergarten, so it has become a natural thing to do.

Second, while we advocate teaching decision making one-on-one, there are many decision opportunities where the whole family can participate, and your younger children can learn from the older ones in the family. For instance, deciding where to go out to eat, where to go on the family trip, or what movie you are going to see are all opportunities to strengthen the family's decision-making skills as well as assess how well your children are embracing them.

Third, especially for younger children, you may want to use make-believe play situations involving their favorite toys or stuffed animals to help them to learn FIVE-to-Decide. As we noted earlier in the book, children's stories are full of examples of opportunities where the decisions being made can be reviewed with your son or daughter, and where using the FIVE-to-Decide lyrics can be used to great effect.

Fourth, use lots of supportive language when discussing decisions. Another friend of ours tells us that she makes sure that she tells her children about how well she likes the way they make decisions. This helps to positively reinforce good decision-making habits. Tell your children when they make a good decision or when faced with a hard decision, that you are confident that they can make a good decision. If they make a mistake, ask how they are going to correct it.

Finally, help them understand that not every "good decision" has "good outcomes." This is a lesson that life has taught us as adults, sometimes cruelly, but it is something that children, teenagers, and many young adults haven't yet experienced. Further, there are going to be decisions where the payoffs are not going to be known for quite some time. Again, as adults we realize this but our children do not—yet. Work within your child's maturity and experience level. It is easy sometimes to forget that they are not "miniature adults," so don't expect too much too soon.

Empowering Your Children

The news is filled with young adults having problems adjusting to college, or worse, life after college. So many parents have focused, even from a young age, on getting their children into the right college that they forget that their role is to prepare their children for life—not school.

For example, in a recent conversation with a college engineering professor, he noted that it was distressing to him that so many of his undergraduate as well as graduate students could only cope with "academic exercises." If he gave them real world problems that had no clear-cut solutions—which most engineering problems have—the students were totally clueless as to what to do. He said that many of his students cannot make decisions when faced with uncertainties or ambiguities. They had never been given a chance either, since their whole life had been scripted from an early age, with their parents making all their decisions for them. In essence, his students had never been given any real decision equity.

It does you little good to instruct your children in decision making if you won't let them make real decisions and realize their consequences. Remember, decision empowerment has two fundamental components—creating the capability in your child to make a good decision and giving them the power to make decisions and the responsibility for their outcomes. One without the other is not decision empowerment but decision impoverishment.

By giving them power over their own decisions—appropriate for their decision-making skill, experience, and emotional maturity—you give your child a lifetime gift that will help them grow into responsible adults with whom you can hold meaningful conversations for as long as you live.

Summary

Only you can teach your child to be a good decision maker because no one else is going to.

Index